# THE
# World
## OF
# Meaning

*A Rediscovery of Purpose*

Christopher Zurcher

The World of Meaning: A Rediscovery of Purpose
©2024 Christopher Zurcher

Published by Clovercroft Publishing, Franklin, Tennessee
www.clovercroftpublishing.com

Edited by Adept Content Solutions

Cover and Interior Design by Jonathan Lewis

Printed in the United States of America

ISBN: 978-1-956370-30-0 (print)

*To Mom and Dad—thank you for always believing in me*

*and*

*To Dr. Jordan Peterson—witnessing your courage has inspired me to search for mine. May your room be forever spotless.*

# Table of Contents

## APPENDICES

# Preface

How do you talk about something that can't be put into words? You talk around it. Or maybe you represent it through dance, music, art, drama—anything that gets the point across.

The nature of man has always been to explore new lands, travel the world, and conquer the unknown. But not all lands exist within a physical space, and the greatest of all explorations has yet to be undertaken—that is, the internal exploration of who we are, where we came from, and the purpose of life. This conceptual land is a place where few have gone, and those who have find it very difficult to put what they have discovered into words. This is the new frontier waiting to be discovered, and it will only be found by those who are brave enough to stare into the abyss.

I grew up attending church and reading the Bible, but the older I got, the more I struggled with Christianity. It just didn't make sense to me; no matter how badly I wanted to, I could not force myself to believe in something that seemed so far-fetched and objectively unreasonable. I then decided that what I was looking for could not be found in church—that as a whole, Christianity was a fairy tale believed by those who were either too naive to know better or too afraid to question their beliefs.

After casting aside what I believed to be my childhood superstitions, I found I had developed an intense thirst to discover the truth about life, and as a result, began experimenting with different spiritual practices in an attempt to get a better handle on what I believed. This eventually led me to Buddhism, where I began buying into the idea that everything was an illusion. I thought myself to be one with the universe, that everything in the universe was moving along to the dictates of its own nature and therefore doing exactly what it needed to be doing. I began to question the concepts of good, bad, right, and wrong—after all, we wouldn't accuse a volcano of being "evil," would we? And although I thought these ideas made more sense than Christianity, I still wasn't satisfied; I still felt empty and hungered for something more.

My search for answers eventually led me to the lectures of Dr. Jordan B. Peterson, clinical psychologist and professor emeritus at the University of Toronto. As I listened to Dr. Peterson lecture, I began to realize that he was talking around/pointing to the very thing I had been searching for. And yet, it seemed like every time I finished a lecture, I could never fully explain what it was I had actually heard. For obvious reasons, this did not sit well with me, and so I made it my mission to understand these ideas the best that I could. In short, I began taking notes during his lectures, and every time I would finish a lecture, I would condense my notes into a small paragraph summarizing the gist of what I had just heard. As a result of rigorously summarizing every lecture I listened to, I saw a through-line. I began to see the bigger picture—a new world—and couldn't believe the profundity of what I had stumbled across.

In this book, I have summarized the ideas of Dr. Jordan B. Peterson and have used them to draw my own conclusions. Therefore, as I go on to explain these ideas, I will often be referencing Dr. Peterson's work (all bold text is a quote from one of Dr. Jordan Peterson's online lectures or podcast episodes and may be slightly modified in an attempt to make it more readable).

There are three parts to this book. Part One will present the problem we are trying to solve, as well as outline different psychological and philosophical theories that indirectly relate to this problem. Part Two will describe the structure of mythology and how our ancestors used these stories to make sense of the world. And finally, using the foundation laid in Parts One and Two, Part Three will attempt to show how the stories of our own culture address the problem laid out in Part One.

Now, as we go through each section, there will be times when it is difficult to understand what these ideas have in common (especially in Parts One and Two). That's okay. The earlier chapters of this book are simply setting the stage. In fact, it's best to think of this book as a puzzle, and each chapter is a piece to that puzzle. And just as it is impossible to see a finished puzzle by looking at a single puzzle piece, we cannot fully understand the scope of these ideas by looking at a single chapter. We must first take each chapter individually, do our best to understand it, and then set it out on the table for later. And it is only after we lay the foundation of our puzzle that we can fill in the remaining pieces and see the resulting image.

The ideas presented in this book have changed my life. I sincerely hope you find what you are looking for.

# Part One

CHAPTER ONE

---

# The Death of God

HAVE YOU NOT HEARD OF that madman who lit a lantern
in the bright morning hours, ran to the market place, and
cried incessantly, "I seek God! I seek God!" As many of those
who do not believe in God were standing around just then,
he provoked much laughter.

Why, did he get lost? said one. Did he lose his way like a
child? said another. Or is he hiding? Is he afraid of us? Has he
gone on a voyage? or emigrated? Thus they yelled and laughed.

The madman jumped into their midst and pierced them
with his glances. "Whither is God," he cried. "I shall tell you.
*We have killed him*—you and I. All of us are his murderers.
But how have we done this? How were we able to drink up
the sea? Who gave us the sponge to wipe away the entire
horizon? What did we do when we unchained this earth from
its sun? Whither is it moving now? Whither are we moving
now? Away from all suns? Are we not plunging continuously?
Backward, sideward, forward, in all directions? Is there any
up or down left? Are we not straying as through an infinite
nothing? Do we not feel the breathe of empty space? Has it
not become colder? Is not night and more night coming on
all the while? Must not lanterns be lit in the morning? Do
we not hear anything yet of the noise of the grave-diggers
who are burying God? Do we not smell anything yet of God's
decomposition? Gods too decompose.

"God is dead. God remains dead. And we have killed him. How shall we, the murderers of all murderers, comfort ourselves? What was holiest and most powerful of all that the world has yet owned has bled to death under our knives. Who will wipe this blood off us? What water is there for us to clean ourselves? What festivals of atonement, what sacred games shall we have to invent? Is not the greatness of this deed too great for us? Must not we ourselves become gods simply to seem worthy of it?"[1]

–Friedrich Nietzsche, *The Parable of the Madman*

The death of God occurred around the time of the Enlightenment—a time when people adopted a more scientific approach to thinking about the world. And although this new interpretation of the world allowed man to vastly improve the conditions of his life, it also came at a cost. As I had done in my own life, the people of the Enlightenment began to view their religious beliefs through a scientific lens and found that they were flawed—a discovery that resulted in the world casting aside what it believed to be superstition for a much more "educated" outlook on life. But the problem is that life is hard; being alive means that we will inevitably face diseases, natural disasters, and even the maliciousness of other human beings—we know that one day we will eventually die, and even worse, we know this to be true for everyone we love. So how could we possibly continue on, knowing this fate awaits us? In the past, it was largely people's religious beliefs that gave them *a purpose*—a reason to persevere through their suffering. But without such a purpose, what hope do we have left?

One thing Friedrich Nietzsche predicted would happen as a result of God's death was the emergence of nihilism,[2] the belief that everything is meaningless. Nihilism is a philosophy that looks at the world and reduces humanity to bacteria growing on a rock. It claims that our world is nothing but a speck of dust among many, floating in a cold, infinite universe. Nihilism says, *In the grand scheme of things, what does it matter? In a million years, who is going to care?*

And once we adopt an attitude of nihilism, we become trapped, cornered into accepting this view of the world. But if life has no meaning, then that means we are suffering for no reason. And if we are suffering for no reason, why continue? As French novelist and philosopher, Albert Camus, once noted, "There is but one truly serious philosophical problem, and that is suicide."

If life has no point, why not kill ourselves? Or better yet why not constantly seek after the attainment of impulsive pleasures—*even at the expense of others*—and then kill ourselves? After all, morality only makes sense if there is a God. Before the death of God, people took morality very seriously because there was a metaphysical idea behind it. But if God does not exist, why does it matter what we do? Why not lie, cheat, rape, steal, or murder to get what we want—*in a million years, who will care?*

By shackling ourselves to a scientific interpretation of the world, we have chosen to throw away something of tremendous value. We have chosen to throw away God and, as a result, have locked ourselves in a prison from which we cannot escape. How trivial it all seems now that we know the truth, now that we can clearly see the pointlessness of life.

But the question I would like to pose to you, dear reader, is this—do you think this is true? Is there really no point to our lives, or could we have made a mistake in our logic? Can we really do whatever we want with no repercussions, or is it possible there is more going on behind the scenes? Is God *really* dead, or is He just . . . lost?

CHAPTER TWO

---

# Piaget and Embodied Cognition

KNOWLEDGE IS NOT STATIC, IT is constantly changing and updating. This is because it is impossible for us to perceive everything; and thank god for that. Can you imagine how overwhelming it would be to perceive everything all at once? Life is stressful enough without having to take in the number of times your ceiling fan rotates every second, your neighbors' fight, and the temperature of your coffee all at the same time. Simply put, the world is too big, and there are too many things. Therefore, if we want to perceive anything at all, we first have to make most things irrelevant—this is why you have to ignore everything else in the room before you can read the words on this page.

But how do we know what to perceive and what to ignore? The answer is, we don't, which means at some point we will inevitably overlook something important. This is why some things can be true for decades, only to be disproven overnight by some newly acquired information. Admittedly, this is a weird spot to be in; how do we know if a "truth" is actually true? After all, the last truth we trusted turned out to be a fraud; what makes this new truth any different?

It really all boils down to how we define *truth*, for there are different types of truth. Perhaps the most obvious type of truth is the one we are most familiar with—scientific, and objective truth; the type of truth that says, "One plus one equals two," and "Every water molecule contains one oxygen and two hydrogen atoms ($H_2O$)." But there are other types of truth that are just as valid—that are just as *true*—as scientific and objective truths, although in a different kind of way.

There is an American school of philosophy called *pragmatism* that defines truth based on the practical utility of something. At first, this definition of truth might sound bizarre, when in reality, our culture has become so obsessed with scientific truth that we have forgotten why we value it in the first place. As humans, our main concern is to live in the world—that is, *to get from Point A to Point B*—and the only reason we created science to begin with was to help us accomplish this. Now, the pragmatists are not concerned with absolute truth; they understand our ability to perceive the world is rather limited, and as a result, it stops us from ever seeing the full picture. Therefore, instead of thinking about ideas as absolutes, the pragmatists see them as *tools* for navigating the world. And by definition, *if a tool successfully accomplishes a task, then it is the right tool for the job*; in the same way, if an idea successfully gets us to where we are going—successfully gets us to Point B—then that idea is true enough to be considered "true." Is there a better definition of truth than that? If an idea works when we act it out in the world, doesn't that indicate there must be something true about it? Otherwise, it would not work.

> **"Facts tend to transform across time. If you take a biology course right now, in twenty years much of what you've learned will have turned out to have been wrong. And that's kind of weird because it isn't wrong right now. And you think, 'How can it be wrong in twenty years?' That's a really complicated problem. And in order to solve that problem you kind of have to think of facts like *tools* instead of thinking of them as objective independent realities. Because a bad tool can still work as a tool.[3]**
>
> **"What the pragmatists state is you don't have ultimate knowledge about anything, so your knowledge always**

bottoms out in ignorance. Then the question is, how do you know if anything is true? And the pragmatists would say, in a sense, you don't; *what you know is if something is true enough for a particular function.* So, for example, your theory about getting to the door might be that you can stand up and walk there. God only knows what might happen on the way there. Maybe there will be an earthquake, or a ceiling tile will fall on you. Who knows? Maybe you'll have a heart attack. You don't *know* whether you can get there . . . but if you get there what you can say is, 'My statement about truth was sufficient so that the outcome was what the theory predicted.' . . . It doesn't require for you to be omniscient about anything for things to be 'true enough.'"[4]

Now, there was a psychologist named Jean Piaget who recognized that this was the case; he wasn't interested in studying facts because he understood that facts change. So, then he asked himself, "Is there anything that *doesn't* change; is there anything that could be considered a real fact?" And after spending some time mulling over the question, Piaget realized that although facts change, the one thing that doesn't is the manner in which people *generate* facts; the *process* people use to acquire new information and transform knowledge itself.[5] This realization led Piaget to study the cognitive development of children from infancy to adulthood; he figured if he could understand how children learn, then he might be able to understand how this fact-generating process developed in humans over time.

In his book *Play, Dreams, and Imitation in Childhood*,[6] Piaget breaks down the cognitive development of children into 4 stages:

1. Sensorimotor stage (0–2 years old)

This is the stage where babies learn by interacting with the world. A baby will begin with simple reflexes, such as sucking or grasping, and then begin developing habits like thumb sucking. Next, the baby becomes aware of objects that exist outside of its body and begins playing with these objects. And as the baby grows older, it begins to explore the world; it learns to sit, crawl, stand, walk, and eventually run.

2. Preoperational stage (2–7 years old)

In the preoperational stage, children begin to understand that words, images, and gestures are actually symbols that can represent something else. For example, a drawing of a stick figure represents a human being and holding your arms out wide means "give me a hug." Next, the child's imagination begins to develop, and they begin to play games and make believe.

3. Concrete operational stage (7–11 years old)

In the third stage of development, children begin to think more logically, and begin to understand the world does not revolve around them; that there are more points of view besides their own.

4. Formal operational stage (12+ years old)

In the fourth and final stage of development, humans become more rational and abstract thinkers and, therefore, can philosophize about complex things.

Interestingly enough, Piaget didn't care too much about the specifics of each stage but was more concerned with the bigger picture—namely, he wanted to understand how someone could transform from a baby into a full-fledged, rational human being. He thought that if he could understand how babies transformed into adults, then he could determine how this fact-generating process developed in humans over time.

## Embodied Cognition

While studying children, the first thing Piaget noticed was how important our bodies were for understanding the world; that we absolutely *needed* bodies if we were going to understand anything at all. For example, our understanding of what something is—whether it is hot, cold, hard, soft, liquid, solid, etc.—depends solely on how our bodies interact with it.[7] And not only that, but we also need our bodies to understand what things mean—for what something *means* is really to say what it *means for action.*

> "When people were first developing models of artificial intelligence they thought they'd be able to develop machines that sort of modeled the world, *and then* would figure out how to act (so abstractly). . . . But that proved to be impossible. . . . And so some robotics engineers started building robots from the bottom-up. They had these mindless robots that were action oriented. The first robots built were these little insect things that could skitter away from light; that's all they could do. Turn on a light—poof!—they'd go find some dark. To that robot, the world was a binary place; it was either a 'light place' or a 'dark place.' And then you might say, 'What did light or dark *mean* to this little robot?' . . . To this robot, light meant *move to a different place.* So that robot was transforming one form of information (light vs. dark), into another form which was *skitter away.* I love that because it's not easy to understand what meaning means until you relate it to the body. And so, Piaget's fundamental proposition is that the elements of your understanding are not perceptual abstractions. In fact, there are even elements of understanding that underlie your perceptual abstractions that are *more* fundamental. And those are essentially your sensory motor skills—*things you do with your body.* It's a lovely idea. It's extremely profound. And I think it's absolutely correct."[8]

The main idea here is that our bodies come first and give us a foundation for understanding the world, a foundation upon which we can build and eventually develop more abstract ideas. For example, think about what it means to be a good person; ultimately, "good person" is an abstract concept rooted in behavior. Imagine, what sort of things make up a good person? Perhaps a good person is someone who is a good neighbor, a good spouse, a good parent, etc.—all things that are abstract concepts themselves. But we can also break *these* abstractions down by asking, "Well, what sort of things make up a 'good parent?'" And we might find that a good parent is someone who makes dinner for the family, or perhaps he or she helps the kids with their homework, or maybe he or she even disciplines the children when it is appropriate. Which then leads us to wonder what it means to "make dinner for the family?" Maybe it means to buy groceries, or to cook the food; maybe it means to set the table for a nice family dinner. And what would "setting the table" entail, you ask? More than likely picking up a fork, knife, and spoon and placing them on the table. And how is that done? *By moving your hand in such a way that allows you to pick up utensils and place them on the table.*[9] And now, here we are; this is how abstract concepts are rooted in action; how the mind meets the body.[10] Ultimately, to understand this is not only to acknowledge how important our bodies are for thinking abstractly, but it is also to recognize that moral abstractions such as "good parent"—an abstraction relating to how we *should behave*—can never be determined through science, as moral abstractions are not scientific categories (descriptions of the world), but rather, pragmatic categories (categories based on action).[11] **(See Fig. 2.1 for an illustration of this process.)**

By studying the cognitive development of children, Piaget learned how important our bodies were for understanding the world; that it was our bodies that laid a foundation for abstract thought. And as he watched children interact in the world, he began noticing how they used their bodies to slowly build themselves into adults through the art of *imitation*. He observed that an infant was born with simple reflexes, but after a period of trial and error, would learn which behaviors successfully accomplished a task, and then would *imitate* those behaviors in the future in order to repeat that success. And once that infant grew into a child, Piaget then saw that this imitation continued, but now, the child would not only imitate their *own* successful behaviors, but also the successful behaviors of other people. In fact, this is how children learn to talk—of course, some explicit instruction may take place, but ultimately, children learn to talk by listening to other people and imitating the sounds they hear![12] Thus, it was the belief of Piaget that children built themselves into adults from the bottom-up, that comprehension began in the body, and only later would it make its way up into the conscious mind.

This theory has some profound implications. For example, imagine a little girl playing house and pretending to be a mother; how does

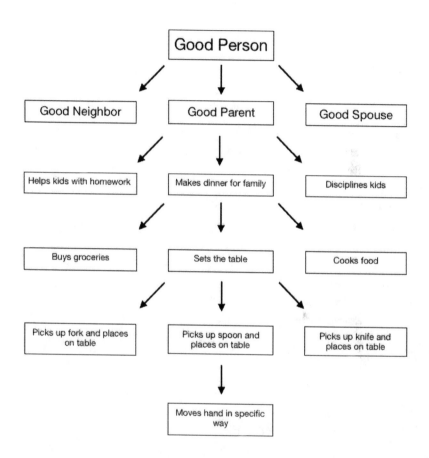

Figure 2.1

this little girl know what to do? First, she watches many mothers act and determines which behaviors are common across all mothers, then she extracts out this "generalized mother behavior" and embodies something like *the spirit of the mother*.[13] Now, of course, when asked what it means to be a mother, this little girl will more than likely not be able to give a coherent answer, but this doesn't stop her from being able to flawlessly act it out. *Fundamentally, this means our ability to imitate allows us to embody more information than we consciously understand.* And if we think about it, of course this is the case. In our example, this little girl is imitating the behavior of mothers who have actually experienced motherhood; these women have learned certain truths about motherhood and have incorporated those truths into their behavior. And so, although this little girl has never experienced motherhood herself, when she imitates the essence of motherhood she unconsciously embodies a vast amount of experience and wisdom.

> We know *how* . . . long before we *know how* we know how, or *why* we know how. This is to say, for example, that a child learns to *act* appropriately (assuming it does) long before it can provide abstracted explanations for or descriptions of its behavior. A child can be "good" without being a moral philosopher.[14]

Because we cannot fully perceive the world in its entirety, our understanding of life is very tool-like in nature.[15] As children, we imitated the people around us and built ourselves from the bottom-up, and as adults, not much has changed. Humans are extremely imitative creatures; we are constantly observing the world and learning new things through our capacity to imitate. We imitate our parents, friends, coworkers, TV characters, and even popular culture. Don't believe me? Why exactly do we put up Christmas trees every year; nothing about this behavior makes any sense—*you are putting a tree in your living room!*

In a sense, humans are one big byproduct of imitation. We acted in the world before we knew how we were acting. We imitated ourselves, as well as those around us, which then led to us embodying more information than we could consciously understand. But those who we imitated—people like our parents—also learned by imitating those who came before them. *This means that we are actually an embodied representation of history itself;* a compilation of behaviors that have worked well in the past. And if this is true, then it also means we are unconsciously acting out ideas that have taken *hundreds of thousands of years* to develop. And what are these ideas? Well, that is what we are still trying to figure out.

## The Cognitive Development of Mankind

In a nutshell, Piaget believed the cognitive development of children started in the body and gradually worked its way up to the conscious mind—a theory that can also be applied, interestingly enough, to the cognitive development of our species as a whole. After all, evolutionary theory suggests that the earliest stages of our development were prelinguistic, meaning that before we could consciously think explicit thoughts, we used our bodies to act in the world.

As the theory goes, our earliest human ancestors first began by acting in the world. And as a result of constantly interacting with each other, they began to learn which behaviors were acceptable, and in what context; that is, they began to interact with each other according to an implicit set of rules. This ultimately led to the manifestation of *games*—social interactions that are governed by a set of rules. If you think about it, all interactions between people are game-like in nature because we are all essentially playing some sort of role within a social setting. For example, during the day we might play the lawyer game, while at night, the parent or spouse game—three vastly different games, each requiring its own set of behaviors, each governed by its own set of rules.

Now, as time progressed, the games we were playing eventually evolved into *rituals*, meaning they became unconscious, automatic, and habitual through repetition. But before we get into ritualized games, it might be helpful to quickly go over ritualized behaviors. Imagine an infant trying to pick up a cup. At first, they will make many attempts, but once they learn how to do it successfully, they will repeat this behavior until it becomes second nature; that is, until this behavior becomes *ritualized*. In the same way, the games we play with one another can also become so ingrained in our bodies that they become second nature. Ritualized games are everywhere if you know where to look; it's how we smile and nod to strangers when we pass them on the street; it's how we stand, how we talk, and how we laugh when we are trying to impress a member of the opposite sex; it is every little unconscious behavior that manifests when we are trying to behave properly and not upset the status quo. And once the games that our ancestors were playing became ritualized, they were then imitated, and passed down through generations as a result.

Next, we began to watch ourselves act; we began to observe the games we were playing and noticed there were certain patterns of behavior that would consistently manifest within those games. Of course, we couldn't exactly say what it was we were noticing because we didn't have the words yet, so instead, we attempted to communicate these ideas the only way we knew how—*with our bodies*. And it was this reenactment of behavioral patterns that turned out to be the beginning stages of *drama*. And once drama had officially emerged, it was only a matter of time before we developed language and could layer these dramas with a narrative structure, thus, transforming them into *stories*. Ultimately, this means there are behavioral patterns containing hundreds of thousands of years of pragmatic wisdom embedded deep within ancient stories; and like a little girl acting out the spirit of motherhood, these stories inevitably contain more information than we consciously know.

[It could be said that the words of a story merely act as a retrieval cue for information we already know but have yet to transform into explicit knowledge.] It is for this reason that Shakespeare might be viewed as a precursor to Freud (think of Hamlet): Shakespeare "knew" what Freud later "discovered," but he knew it more implicitly, more imagistically, more procedurally. (This is not to say Shakespeare was any less brilliant, just that his level of abstraction was different.) Ideas after all, come from somewhere; they do not arise, spontaneously, from the void. Every complex psychological theory has a lengthy period of historical development (development that might not be evidently linked to the final emergence of the theory).[16]

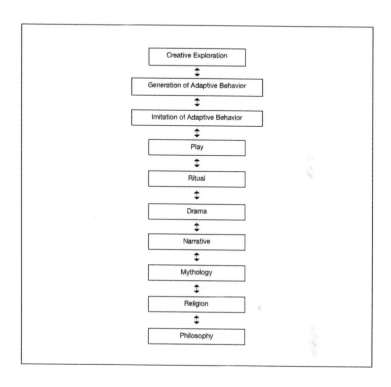

Figure 2.2

And as we told each other stories, the best and most compelling of these stories were *mythologized* while the remaining stories faded away. And once mythology was established, we then took the lessons (morality) found in these stories and built religions around them. And finally, we eventually learned to rationally critique the religions we were practicing, which ultimately allowed us to consciously alter our behavior moving forward **(See Fig 2.2 for an illustration of this process.)**[17]

> Behavior is imitated, then abstracted into play, formalized into drama and story, crystalized into myth and codified into religion—and only then criticized in philosophy, and provided, *post-hoc*, with rational underpinnings. Explicit philosophical statements regarding the grounds for and nature of ethical behavior, stated in a verbally comprehensible manner, were not established through rational endeavor.[18]

First, we acted in the world. Then we began to tell stories about how we were acting and used these stories as the basis for religion. But one day we woke up and questioned how we were doing things; we looked at these stories and unanimously decided that they could not possibly be true. But because these ancient stories are based on the pragmatic behaviors of our species, they contain more information, more wisdom, and more *truth* than we could possibly understand; it is just that they contain a different type of truth than we are currently use to.

## Recap

- Pragmatism defines truth based on the practical utility of something. Therefore, the pragmatists believe ideas should be treated as *tools* for navigating the world.
- Having a body is vital for comprehending the world.
- Moral abstractions are rooted in behavior and therefore belong to pragmatic categories instead of scientific categories.
- Our ability to imitate allows us to embody more information than we can consciously understand.
- Children act first and then build themselves from the bottom-up. This theory of cognitive development can also be applied to how

the human species developed: mankind acted in the world first, and then built themselves from the bottom-up.

- The cognitive development of mankind goes as follows: creative exploration - imitation - playing games - ritual - drama - narrative - mythology - religion - philosophy.

- As a species, we are currently acting out more information—more ideas—than we consciously understand. These ideas—these pragmatic *truths*—are rooted deep within our historical past and have been preserved through ancient stories.

# CHAPTER THREE

# Phenomenology

AT THE END OF THE day, all ideas are based on a set of assumptions, that is, certain things we must first accept as being true before an idea can make any sense. Because it is impossible for us to know everything, we have to assume some things are true in order to act in the world with confidence—which is why the pragmatists believed ideas should be thought of as tools, as opposed to absolute truths.

Now, if ideas are tools based on a set of assumptions, then that means we might be able to change our assumptions and develop new tools—perhaps even better tools—for navigating the world. For example, for over a thousand years, people believed Euclidean geometry described the world perfectly. But before using Euclidean geometry, you first had to adopt a set of mathematical assumptions. Then in the later part of the nineteenth century, a new form of geometry was invented based on an entirely different set of assumptions, and this new form of geometry not only seemed to describe the world better, but it also turned out to be the exact type of geometry Einstein needed to develop some of his groundbreaking theories.[19]

It might be safe to say that because the world is such a complicated place, the more tools we have for navigating it, the better. But before we can create new tools, we must first change how we think about the world—that is, we must change the underlying set of assumptions we have grown so accustomed to.

## Changing Our Assumptions: The Scientific Lens

It seems like people today are only comfortable viewing the world through a scientific lens. But they forget that the scientific lens, like all ideas, is based on an assumption; namely, that the material world existed first and, therefore, everything that exists is a byproduct of a more fundamental material reality.

The scientific lens would have us believe that the material world is the most fundamental reality that exists, and that everything else—all nonmaterial things like consciousness and the meanings we experience—is some sort of illusion that can easily be explained by material properties. This is mainly due to the fact that when we look at the world through a scientific lens, meaning doesn't exist. But when looking through this lens, we fail to recognize that this isn't because the world is actually without meaning, it is because the scientific lens was intentionally designed to remove all meaning from the world in the first place so that it could properly conduct experiments.

The goal of a scientist is to come up with theories that explain the world—theories which must be grounded in reality for anyone to take them seriously. But how do scientists know if something is truly grounded in reality? One way this can be determined is by having multiple people conduct the same experiment and see if they get the same results. And if a theory can be consistently repeated with the same results, then it's likely that this theory is grounded in reality.

This rationale gave birth to the scientific method, a method that requires scientists to conduct experiments in a way so that those experiments can be repeated by multiple people. But in order for an experiment to be consistently repeated, these scientists had to remove anything from their experiments that could cause their findings to vary—which means they attempted to remove things like their own personal biases, as well as the subjective meaning/value/motivational significance of objects. *This means that before an experiment even begins, meaning is completely removed from the entire equation!* And once all the meaning has been removed, scientists will then look at the world and claim that meaning is nowhere to be found—implying that meaning is not "real"—all the while forgetting that they were the ones who removed the world's meaning in the first place in order to conduct their experiments.[20]

This is exactly what we do when we observe the world through a scientific lens—we remove all the meaning from an object and then claim that objects don't have any meaning. But this doesn't mean that objects are *actually* without meaning. It just means we removed the meaning before making our observation.

The scientific lens is a very powerful tool, but that doesn't mean it is flawless. It is based on the assumption that the world of objects is our primary reality, and everything else that exists is a byproduct of that material reality. But removing consciousness from the definition of reality might be a huge mistake because it appears that the material world may only "exist" in relation to a conscious observer:

> Things have a nature that appears independent of subjective will, and follow their own laws of being and development—despite our wishes. However, the job of determining what a thing is in the absence of the subject is much more difficult than might initially be imagined. It is certainly the case—as we have seen—that the *value* of an object can shift with shifts in frame of reference. It appears to be true, however, that what an *object* is "is and of itself" is also subject to such shift. Any given object—a table, say—exists *as a table* because it is apprehended only in a very limited and restrained manner. Something is a table at a particular and isolated level of analysis, specified by the nature of the observer. In the absence of this observer, one might ask, what is it that is being apprehended? Is the proper level of analysis and specification subatomic, atomic or molecular (or all three at once)? Should the table be considered an indistinguishable element of the earth upon which it rests, or of the solar system, which contains the earth, or of the galaxy itself? The same problem obtains from the perspective of temporality. What is now table was once tree; before that, earth—before that, rock; before that, star. What is now table also has before it an equally complex and lengthy

developmental history waiting in "front" of it; it will be, perhaps, ash, then earth, then—far enough in the future—part
of the sun again (when the sun finally re-envelops the earth).
The table is what it "is" only at a very narrow span of spatial
and temporal resolution (the span that precisely characterizes
our consciousness). So what is the table as an "independent
object"—"free," that is, of the restrictions that characterize
the evidently limited human viewpoint? . . . Is that "thing"
everything it once was, everything it is, and everything it will
be, all at the same time? Where then are its borders? How
can it be distinguished from other things? And without such
distinction, in what manner can it be said to exist?

Question: what is an object, in the absence of a frame of
reference? Answer: it is everything conceivable, at once—is
something that constitutes the union of all currently discrim-
inable opposites (and something that cannot, therefore, be
easily distinguished from nothing).

I am not saying that there are no such things as "things"—
that would of course be patently absurd. . . . What I am claiming
is that "objective" things are in fact the product of an interaction
between whatever constitutes our limited consciousness and
whatever constitutes the unlimited "background" that makes
up the world, in the absence of a subject.[21]

Consciousness is what appears to give the objective world its
form, and without a conscious observer, it is impossible to know
how things would really "exist." Without a conscious observer
serving as a reference point, the objective world would not have a
size or a shape; it would not have a smell, a color, or a texture; and
perhaps most importantly, it would not have a duration.[22] If there is
no conscious observer to give the objective world its borders, then
there would be no way to distinguish one object from another. And
if there are no singular objects, then there is just *everything* all at
once. And something that is everything all at once cannot "be easily
distinguished from nothing." Therefore, it appears that removing
consciousness from the definition of reality is not as easy as the
scientific lens would have us believe.

# Changing Our Assumptions: Phenomenology

"People confuse the fact that science is value-free (sort of) with the idea that existence is value-free. That's philosophically primitive because science was actually set up to get rid of the subjective value in its technique. So you can't say, 'We set this thing up to get rid of all the value, and look, all the value is gone! There's no value!' It's like no, no, no. *You* put that domain out of the range of consideration. That doesn't mean that value doesn't exist. It means that measuring value requires a different philosophy, a different outlook, different techniques, different tools, different methods of proof."[23]

The scientific lens is a tool for navigating the world, and like all tools, it is based on an assumption. But there are other tools for navigating the world that can be just as useful that are based on entirely different assumptions. And one of those tools, made popular by the German philosopher Martin Heidegger, is called *phenomenology* (say "phenomena," drop the "a" and add "-ology" to the end).

In a nutshell, Heidegger believed that Western philosophy was focusing on the wrong things; he believed that we had become way too concerned with what the world was made out of, and instead, should focus more on how we *experienced* the world. When looking through a scientific lens, we assume that the world of objects is our primary reality and that things like meaning and consciousness are merely symptoms of that reality. But phenomenology flips this assumption on its head; it claims that our primary reality is not the world of objects, but rather, everything that we experience—that is, *the world of meaning.*[24]

According to phenomenology, everything that we experience—our emotions, motivations, dreams, gut feelings, and all meaning—should be thought of as *real*, instead of being brushed aside as some sort of illusion or symptom of the material world. Now, it's important to understand that phenomenologists do not deny objective reality, nor do they claim that our experiences are real like a chair is objectively real. How they define what constitutes "real" is actually based on a completely different set of criteria (something we will discuss more in the next section). This means that the objective definition of real and the phenomenological definition of real belong to different categories of "real" and do not need to conflict with one another.

Admittedly, at first. it's pretty hard to grasp how something that's not objectively real can still be real. This is usually because we are so used to viewing the world through a scientific lens and can't possibly imagine any other way of looking at things. In the next section, we will discuss how it's possible for something to be real without meeting the objective criteria for reality. It's best to treat this as an intellectual exercise; try and detach from the assumption that our primary reality is the material world and see if you can see things through the phenomenological lens.

## The World of Meaning

When we look at the world through a scientific lens, we think that we see objects first and then later determine what those objects mean. For example, we think that when we see a plastic cup we see the cup first and then later infer its meaning: *something to drink out of.* But the phenomenologists flip this assumption around; they claim that we see meaning first and then infer the material object—that is, they believe that when we see a plastic cup, we first perceive *something to drink out of,* and then afterwards perceive the cup.[25]

The main reason phenomenologists believe that we see meaning first is that, as humans, our primary concern is to survive in the world in the world, which means that it is more helpful to know what things *mean for action* instead of what they are objectively made out of.

> It is not enough to know that something *is.* It is equally necessary to know what it *signifies.* It might even be argued that animals—and human beings—are *primarily* concerned with the affective or emotional significance of the environment.
>
> Along with our animal cousins, we devote ourselves to fundamentals: will this (new) thing eat me? Can I eat it? Will it chase me? Should I chase it? Can I mate with it? We *may* construct models of "objective reality," and it is no doubt useful to do so. We *must* model meanings, however, in order to survive.[26]

In order to survive in the world, it appears our brains have evolved to see meaning first.[27] If we walk to the edge of a cliff, we don't actually see a cliff, we see *a falling off place* because that is what we need to know in order to survive. In fact, it might actually be the case that the most real thing about a cliff is that you can fall off of it.[28]

Therefore, if our brains have evolved to see meaning first, and seeing meaning has kept us alive, is there anything more real than meaning?[29] The meanings we experience are real—perhaps even more real than the material world—because they contain information about how we should act; and how we should act towards something is a better indication of what that something actually is.

## I. Acceptance Letter[30]

Imagine your life's goal is to attend Harvard University because it is a family tradition. Everyone in your family went to Harvard—your parents, your grandparents, even your older siblings are currently attending Harvard classes. So in order to keep this tradition alive, you decide to dedicate yourself to your schoolwork. You go above and beyond on all your homework, tests, and projects. You even take up multiple extracurricular activities so that you can separate yourself from the competition. As you dedicate yourself to your life's goal, the years quickly pass by, and the day eventually comes where you finally apply to Harvard.

One day, as you wait to hear back, you see the mailman leaving your house. Your heart starts racing. Is today the day? You sprint to the mailbox and pull out a big envelope with the Harvard insignia printed on the front. All the blood rushes to your head, and your body begins pumping full of adrenaline; a mixture of excitement and panic overwhelms you as you rush back towards the house screaming for your parents to join you in opening the letter.

Now, in this moment, what are you holding in your hands? Are you simply holding a piece of paper with ink on it, or are you holding something more? From the scientific perspective, this is just a piece of paper. But if it is *just* a piece of paper, then why is your heart racing? And if it is just a piece of paper, then why are you running around the house screaming at the top of your lungs? The answer is: because this is *not* just a piece of paper. From the phenomenological perspective, what you are holding is not a piece of paper, but instead, *a portal* to different realities. This piece of paper will not only determine your future (will you keep up the family tradition by becoming a Harvard student, or will you become the family outcast), but it will also determine your past (what exactly were you doing when you were studying to become a Harvard student if you don't actually get into Harvard?).

Is this piece of paper a portal, scientifically speaking? No. Scientifically speaking, this piece of paper is only a piece of paper. But as the phenomenologists point out, we don't live in the world of objects—or at least the objective world is not our primary reality. *Our primary reality is the world of meaning.* When you look at that piece of paper, you don't really perceive a piece of paper—you perceive what that piece of paper *means*. You actually experience this piece of paper as a door to different realities, and the phenomenologists believe that this experience is *real* because it informs you about what this piece of paper actually is! Therefore, by opening that envelope, you are walking through a portal into an entirely different reality, and the anticipation of that journey has caused your heart to pound and your body to fill with adrenaline.

Think about what happens, for example, when you stop by the mailbox and pick up your mail. Consider, as well, what that mail is "made of." Materially speaking, it is merely paper and ink. But that material substrate is essentially irrelevant. It would not matter if the message was delivered by email or voice—or in Morse code, for that matter. What is relevant is the content. And that means that each piece of mail is a container of content—of potential or information, positive, neutral, or negative. Maybe, for example, it is a notification of investigation from your country's tax department. This means that, despite its apparently harmless presence in your hand, the letter is tightly and inextricably connected to a gigantic, complex and oft-arbitrary structure that may well not have your best interests in mind. Alternatively, perhaps it is something joyful, such as an unexpected letter from someone loved or a long-awaited check. From such a perspective, an envelope is a container—a mysterious container, at least in potential—from which an entire new world might emerge.[31]

## II. Twin Towers[32]

On September 11, 2001, two commercial airplanes were hijacked by terrorists and flown into the North and South Towers of the World Trade Center in New York City, killing thousands of people.

Do you remember where you were when you first heard the news? Do you remember how you felt? Were you in shock? Were you scared? Were you angry, sad, or confused? Perhaps you were all of these at the same time. Now, with that in mind, consider this: what exactly was it that fell on September 11, 2001? Were those *buildings* that fell? Or was it something more?

From the scientific perspective, buildings were the only things that fell that day. But if it was only buildings that fell, why were we so shocked? And why did the whole world stop and watch in horror? It's because these buildings were not just isolated objects standing in a deserted field in the middle of nowhere. What fell did not just exist in the world of objects, it also existed in the world of meaning, and represented something much more complicated than mere buildings.

"**The people who took the towers down weren't trying to knock buildings down . . .** *they were trying to knock down the things the buildings were invisibly related to.* **And then you might ask, 'What were those buildings invisibly related to?' And you could actually reverse the question and say, 'Well, what** *weren't* **they related to?' And the reason that people were traumatized in the aftermath of the attacks was because when our bodies answered that question, the answer was, 'Uh oh! Those buildings were probably attached to everything in every possible way.' And so God only knows what's going to come leaping out of that.**"[33]

When the twin towers fell we were left with many unanswered questions: What does this mean for the economy? What does this mean for politics? How is the world going to respond to this? Will there be more attacks? Am I safe? Are the people I love safe? Will we go to war? If we go to war, what will that mean for my life and the life of my family? To describe what fell on September 11, 2001, as "buildings" is not fully correct. When the towers fell that day, what really fell was an invisible layer of security and protection, and what emerged in its place was a near infinite number of unknown potential threats. And it was this loss of security and emergence of potential danger that we experienced in our bodies—an experience that a phenomenologist would consider to be real because that was exactly what was happening; it just wasn't happening in the objective material world.

Phenomenology claims the meanings we experience are real because they inform us about things that are *really* occurring. That means our emotions are real, our dreams are real, our gut feelings are real; it means that everything we experience is a real phenomenon and should not be discounted and explained away on scientific grounds. To do so would be like claiming a grieving mother who had just lost a child in a car accident was only grieving because there were certain chemicals being released in her brain. If you made that claim, you wouldn't be wrong, scientifically speaking. But you most certainly would not be right.

## Meaning Shines Forth

> "There are different ways of thinking about what the world is made out of. We think that it's made out of matter—that's the basic dogma of the materialist realm. I would say it's *really* useful to treat the world as if it's made out of matter; look at all the things that treating it that way has allowed us to do. But that doesn't mean it's the final statement about the nature of reality . . . We also act as if things other than matter are real. So, for example, we act as if potential is real . . . And I would say most of the time when we are dealing with the world, what we are dealing with is not the material world, per se, what we are dealing with is potential; we are dealing with what things *could* be."[34]

We don't just live in the material world, we also live in the world of meaning. And so, when we go about our day, we are not only interacting with objects, but we are also interacting with the meanings that emerge from these objects. Meaning is a weird thing because it is not something we can consciously summon with sheer willpower; we can't just choose what we find meaningful, it is something that chooses us. Meaning is something we encounter, something we experience; it is something that grabs our attention and doesn't let go. The word *phenomena* comes from the Greek word *phainesthai*, which means "to shine forth, to appear, or to be brought to light."[35] And when we experience meaning that is exactly how we experience it—as something that makes itself known to us. For example, when you walk through a bookstore, you might say something like, "That book caught my eye," or "It jumped out at me."[36] But what does that mean? It means that out of all the books you could have noticed, that specific book *grabbed your attention*; a meaning shined forth to you through an object (the book) and pulled your interest forward.

This raises two questions: Why do some things present themselves to us as meaningful while others do not? And second, if we followed these meanings, where exactly would they lead?

## Recap

- Ideas are tools for navigating the world. All ideas are based on a set of assumptions. If we change our assumptions, we can create new tools for navigating the world.
- The scientific lens is based on the assumption that our primary reality is the world of objects. Phenomenology is based on the assumption that our primary reality is the world of meaning (everything we experience).
- Meaning is real because it can inform us about things that are really occurring.
- In order to survive, humans have evolved to see meaning first, which means the world of meaning is our primary reality. And because meaning has kept us alive, it might be the case that meaning is the most real thing we will ever come into contact with.
- Objective reality and phenomenological reality belong to different categories of real and therefore do not conflict or disprove one another.
- Meaning shines forth to us through the material world and grabs our attention.

# CHAPTER FOUR

---

# Carl Rogers

CARL ROGERS WAS AN AMERICAN psychologist who helped develop something called the humanistic approach to psychology, a form of psychology that focuses on treating people like unique individuals, as opposed to machine parts that can be fixed with some cookie-cutter diagnosis.

Rogers believed that every individual had a deep desire to reach their full potential, and because every individual is unique, the pathway to reaching that potential was specific to them. Now, because Rogers believed the pathway to reaching our full potential was specific to us, he thought the only way we could reach this potential was by staying true to ourselves. Meaning, we must fully embrace who we are and represent ourselves truthfully in our thoughts, speech, and actions.

But attaining this state of truth is not always easy. Being true to ourselves means we might not always fit in or be accepted by our peers. And so, in order to avoid this conflict, we sometimes deny and distort parts of ourselves; we lie to ourselves, as well as to the world, and pretend to be something we are not.

According to Rogers, whenever we are not being true to ourselves, we experience a contradiction in personality; that is, we experience a mismatch between who we truly are—how we experience the world—and who we claim to be. And because we cannot be one person and someone else at the same time, Rogers believed this mismatch would cause us to be at odds with ourselves, and would result in anxiety, distress, and other forms of negative emotion. And this negative emotion was an indication that we were veering off the path leading to our full potential.

Carl Rogers referred to this contradiction in personality as *incongruence* and believed it was one of the main causes of pathology in the individual. He believed our willingness to falsify our own experience—*our willingness to lie*—led to unnecessary suffering, and the only way we could untangle these internal contradictions, and therefore reach our full potential, was to live in truth.

## Our Sixth Sense

Think about how we use words. Most of us use words to get what we want from other people. We find ourselves thinking things like, "How should I phrase this sentence in order to appeal to this person; what should I say to give myself the best chance of getting what I want?"[37] Maybe we use our words to impress someone. Or maybe we use them to win an argument. Regardless of the reason, whenever we use words in this manner, we are engaging in something referred to as *instrumental speech*—speech used to manipulate the world in hopes of achieving a desired outcome—and have refused to represent ourselves truthfully.

> You can use words to manipulate the world into delivering what you want. This is what it means to "act politically." This is spin. It's the specialty of unscrupulous marketers, salesmen, advertisers, pickup artists, slogan-possessed utopians and psychopaths. It's the speech people engage in when they attempt to influence and manipulate others. It's what university students do when they write an essay to please the professor, instead of articulating and clarifying their own ideas. It's what everyone does when they want something, and decide to falsify themselves to please and flatter. It's scheming and sloganeering and propaganda.
>
> To conduct life like this is to become possessed by some ill-formed desire, and then to craft speech and action in a manner that appears likely, rationally, to bring about that end.

Typical calculated ends might include "to impose my ideological beliefs," "to prove that I am (or was) right," to appear competent," 'to ratchet myself up the dominance hierarchy," "to avoid responsibility" (or its twin, "to garner credit for others' actions"), "to be promoted," "to attract the lion's share of attention," "to ensure that everyone likes me," "to garner the benefits of martyrdom," "to justify my cynicism," "to rationalize my antisocial outlook," "to minimize immediate conflict," "to maintain my naïveté," "to capitalize on my vulnerability," "to always appear as the sainted one," or (this one is particularly evil) "to ensure that it is always my unloved child's fault." These are all examples of what Sigmund Freud's compatriot, the lesser-known Austrian psychologist Alfred Adler, called "life-lies."[38]

When we use speech instrumentally, we are deceiving the world about our true intentions—that is, we are choosing to lie about who we are and what we want. But this kind of deception is not only limited to speech, Rogers also believed we could act out falsehoods.[39] If our minds can create false representations of ourselves, then it only makes sense that we can act these false representations out in the world—all this is to say that Rogers thought *we could embody a lie*. And it was these two type of lies—the lies we speak and the lies we act out—that Rogers believed caused a contradiction in personality and resulted in unnecessary suffering. Therefore, in order to avoid this contradiction, Rogers thought we must speak and act in ways that accurately reflect who we are and how we are experiencing the world.

But how do we do this when half the time we don't even know what the truth is? The first thing we must do is *pay attention*; put simply, we cannot be true to our experiences if we don't know what those experiences are. As you go about your day, observe how the things you say and do make you feel. Rogers believed that we had a sixth sense—an instinct—that would alert us to whenever we were being inauthentic to ourselves.[40] He believed that whenever we were engaging in a lie, we could actually feel the incongruence occurring in our bodies in the form of an uneasy sensation that would make us feel hollow and weak. And once we felt that sensation, we could immediately stop what it was that we were doing and change course.

> **"You sort of have to detach yourself from your thoughts and what you say. You start by assuming what you say and what you think are not necessarily you. And of course, that's the case because most of what you think and say are the opinions of other people—they are either things you've read or things people have told you.**[41] **You listen to yourself like you would listen to someone else. And then think, 'Do I actually believe that? Is that actually *my* thought?' And what you'll find is 95% of what you say has nothing to do with you.**[42]
>
> **"My sense has been you can tell when you are saying something that's not authentic by feeling out whether it makes you feel weak or strong. . . . Watch for two weeks and see. Make a rule to shut up if you start to say something and it makes you feel weak—to me, that means I can feel things coming apart sort of in my midsection . . . like I've just stepped off solid ground onto something that doesn't support me well, and it feels like a self-betrayal. When that happens the rule is, *shut up*. If that happens, stop talking! And then feel around and see if you can find some words that won't produce that sensation."**[43]

According to Carl Rogers, it is the falsification of our unique individual experiences—*our commitment to the lie*—that makes people sick. But he also believed that if we paid attention and responded truthfully in speech and action to the meanings we experienced, then that would allow us to reach our full potential as individuals, and heal us of all unnecessary suffering.

## Recap

- When we misrepresent ourselves—when we lie—it causes a contradiction in personality, which then leads to unnecessary suffering.
- Rogers believed we had a sixth sense that alerted us to when this

contradiction was taking place; he believed that our bodies informed us when we were engaging in a lie.

- To combat this contradiction in personality, we must pay attention to the meanings we experience and respond to these meanings as truthfully and authentically as possible.
- Rogers believed that the lie causes suffering and the truth heals.

# CHAPTER FIVE

# Existentialism

WHAT DOES IT MEAN TO believe something? We often hear ideas that sound good and then say that we believe them, but does saying we believe something really mean that we believe it? If we looked at our lives, would we find that our behavior aligns with the things we claim to believe? And if not—if we have beliefs that we don't put into practice—in what way can we say that we actually believe those things?

When we act in the world, we are implicitly making a statement of belief. For example, if I choose to eat a candy bar instead of a salad, I am implicitly telling the world that I believe candy bars are more valuable than salads (at least in that specific moment)—otherwise, I wouldn't have chosen to eat the candy bar. The cliched saying that *actions speak louder than words* immediately comes to mind here, as it seems that our behaviors are truly the best indicator of what we believe to be most valuable.

Now, there is a brand of philosophy called *existentialism* that embraces this idea of beliefs being determined by behavior. For an existentialist, the only way to claim what you believe is to act it out in the world. Period. That is, you don't get to say what you believe, you have to show it. This is why existentialism has been referred to as an *embodied philosophy*—the only way you can claim to believe something is by embodying that belief in your everyday life.

**"The Existential definition of truth is action-predicated. For the existentialists truth is a way of being, not a collection of**

**descriptions ... Nietzsche would say for example, 'It doesn't matter what you say, it matters what you do. And if I want to figure out what you believe, I don't ask you, I watch how you act and I assume your true beliefs are the ones directing your actions.' So truth is discovered in action."**[44]

## The Existential Question

Existentialism is a philosophy that begins by acknowledging the harsh conditions of life and recognizing that these conditions are made even worse by their arbitrariness. There seems to be no rhyme or reason why someone is born into a certain time period, geographical location, social class, or family. Just as there doesn't seem to be an explanation as to why someone is born with bad health or good health. And in many ways, this arbitrariness can lead to even more suffering because it can be perceived as unfair.

Usually, we think that if we are suffering, then there must be something wrong with us. But the existentialists don't see it that way at all. The existentialists view suffering as something similar to a ticket of admission—the price we pay for being alive. They claim that people are pathological not because they did something wrong, but because the conditions of life are so tragic, and the weight of existence so heavy, that pathology is the only outcome and, therefore, the default position for everyone.[45]

Existential philosophy begins with the assumption that the only thing guaranteed in life is suffering. You don't get to not suffer. And given that suffering is a certainty, they then pose the question: is there a way we can live that would not only minimize our suffering but would also produce enough meaning in our lives to make our suffering worth it? Or said another way: is there a way we can live in the world that would make us want to voluntarily embrace our suffering and consider it a reasonable price to pay for being alive?

The existentialists believed the answer to their question could be found in the meanings that we experienced—that is, the meanings that shined forth and grabbed our attention. They believed that these meanings not only informed us about the world, but that they also served as guideposts and would tell us what we should and shouldn't do;[46] that if we paid attention to these meanings and allowed them to guide us through life—that is, if we represented our experiences truthfully—then this would make us strong enough to withstand the arbitrary suffering of life.

But how does following the meanings we experience make us stronger exactly? Well, there will be many times in life when we know something is wrong, but instead of listening to this instinct for meaning, we lie to ourselves and pretend that everything is fine. But if we would only listen to ourselves and face the things we were avoiding, we would effectively be putting ourselves in a position to learn new things. And any time we learn something new, we become more competent and, therefore, stronger.

This is an extremely encouraging idea. Yes, life is hard and full of suffering, but we also could be strong enough to overcome this suffering if we would only choose to do so. By paying attention to the meanings we experience and responding to these meanings truthfully—by choosing to confront the things we are avoiding and not shy away from the truth—the existentialists claim that we will become strong enough to take on the tragedy of our lives.

> "It's the only optimistic hypothesis I've ever seen in psychology.[47] How weak are human beings? Ultimately weak. We are up against the crushing weight of society and nature—in that sense, we are extraordinarily weak. But it turns out if we face that opponent, then all sorts of possibilities manifest themselves inside of us, and it isn't clear what the upper limits are to that . . . The existentialists make the strongest case possible for the vulnerability of human beings, and out of that they make the strongest case possible for why human beings are strong and powerful."[48]

## A Claim to Morality

When we ignore the meanings we experience—when we deceive ourselves about what we know to be true—we set ourselves up to fail. This is because the meanings we experience inform us about the structure of reality and, therefore, help us to better understand

and navigate the world. But when we deceive ourselves, we build a map of the world that doesn't accurately represent the terrain we are navigating. And an inaccurate map will inevitably cause us to bump into things and fall into holes.

When we lie to ourselves about what we are experiencing, we build a map of the world that will eventually cause us to fall. This means that lying to ourselves produces its own punishment. And it is for this reason that the existentialists have labeled lying as *immoral*.

"Existentialists believe there are some things you cannot get away with, and one of them is you fundamentally cannot get away with being immoral. Immoral things are precisely those things you can't get away with, *that's why people have identified them as immoral*—the consequences of enacting them will inevitably be brought to bear on you or on the people you love.[49] You can't get away with deceiving yourself because you need a model of the world that is like the world, or you will just bump into the world. So deception brings it's own punishment and *that's* why it's immoral.[50]

"My experience as a therapist—just so you know—I've never seen anyone get away with anything. I think every time you do something you know isn't right, you're going to get walloped for it sooner or later. Now, you may have blinded yourself so badly with your misapprehensions and deceptions that you can't see the causal connection between what you did and the punishment—in fact, sometimes it takes years of psychotherapeutic investigation to lay out the causal narrative—but why would anybody ever think they can bend the structure of reality and get away with it? To me it's like those plastic rulers. You can hold one of those in front of your nose and bend it forward, and that's fine but as soon as you let go it's going to hit you in the face. Then you're going to curse fate because you got hit in the face. But *you* bent the damn ruler."[51]

Moral relativists believe that morality is a set of arbitrary rules created by society, and that those rules can be anything society wants them to be. But the existentialists aren't interested in that debate. In fact, they completely undercut moral relativism by defining morality in a way so that it is applicable for everyone. The existentialists claim that immoral things are those things in your life that you *could* change, but do not, that end up resulting in outcomes that are catastrophic for you. Essentially, they are claiming that we fundamentally cannot get away with deceiving ourselves,[52] and any attempt to do so, will come at a price.

When we ignore the meanings we experience, we practice lying to ourselves. And the more we lie to ourselves, the easier lying becomes. If we continue to lie, our instinct that tells us when we are lying gets weaker and weaker until we can no longer feel it. This means that lying corrupts the very thing that helps us interpret the world and create accurate maps. And once this instinct has been corrupted, we won't be able to model reality in a way where positive meanings can shine forth. All we will be able to experience as a result of our faulty map making is life's misery and horror. And if misery and horror are the only things we experience, we will get bitter, and resentful, and will seek revenge on the rest of world.[53]

But it doesn't stop there. The lies that destroy us also destroy the world around us. It's pretty common to think that what happened in places like Nazi Germany and the Soviet Union was a result of people following the orders of a few corrupt individuals. But those who were there, and who took the problem seriously, did not blame corrupt leaders for their situation. They blamed the willingness of every individual within those societies to turn a blind eye to the things they knew to be wrong and participate in the lies. They believed it was the lies told by regular, ordinary individuals that led to something so closely resembling hell the differences were trivial.[54]

Now this type of destruction does not happen all at once. It happens slowly, with one lie at a time. It usually begins with something small that bothers us—something we know we should address—but in order to avoid conflict, we convince ourselves that it doesn't matter. And then maybe the next time something bothers us, we are too embarrassed to speak up. And the next time, well, perhaps it's just not the right time for us to say something. And as time goes on and we continue lying about our experience, we eventually turn ourselves into the type of people who are incapable of speaking the truth:

If you say no to your boss, or your spouse, or your mother, when it needs to be said, then you transform yourself into someone who *can* say no when it needs to be said. If you say yes when no needs to be said, however, you transform yourself into someone who can only say yes, even when it is very clearly time to say no. If you ever wonder how perfectly ordinary, decent people could find themselves doing the terrible things the gulag camp guards did, you now have your answer. By the time *no* seriously needed to be said, there was no one left capable of saying it.[55]

One of the things that characterized the communist state was that no one said anything they actually believed. *Ever*.[56] No one told the truth because the truth was dangerous and would get you arrested. A man by the name of Aleksandr Solzhenitsyn, a survivor of the Soviet Union gulag system, wrote about his experiences in those forced labor camps, as well as the conditions that led to such monstrosities:

*The Lie as a Form of Existence.* Whether giving in to fear, or influenced by material self-interest or envy, people can't nonetheless become stupid so swiftly. Their souls may be thoroughly muddied, but they still have a sufficiently clear mind. They cannot believe that all the genius of the world has suddenly concentrated itself in one head with a flattened, low-hanging forehead. They simply cannot believe the stupid and silly images of themselves which they hear over the radio, see in films, and read in newspapers. Nothing forces them to speak the truth in reply, but no one allows them to keep silent! They have to *talk!* And what else but a lie? They have to applaud madly, and no one requires honesty of them.

The permanent lie becomes the only safe form of existence, in the same way as betrayal. Every wag of the tongue can be overheard by someone, every facial expression observed by someone. Therefore every word, if it does not have to be a direct lie, is nonetheless obliged not to contradict the general, common lie. There exists a collection of ready-made phrases, of labels, a selection of ready-made lies. And not one single speech nor one single essay or article nor one single book—be it scientific, journalistic, critical, or "literary," so-called—can exist without the use of these primary clichés. In the most scientific of texts it is required that someone's false authority or false priority be upheld somewhere, and that someone be cursed for telling the truth; without this lie even an academic work cannot see the light of day. And what can be said about those shrill meetings and trashy lunch-break gatherings where you are compelled to vote against your own opinion, to pretend to be glad over what distresses you?

In prison Tenno recalled with shame how two weeks before his own arrest he had lectured the sailors on "The Stalinist Constitution—The Most Democratic in the World." And of course not one word of it was sincere.

There is no man who has typed even one page . . . without lying. There is no man who has spoken from a rostum . . . without lying. There is no man who has spoken into a microphone . . . without lying.

But if only it had all ended there! After all, it went further than that: every conversation with the management, every conversation in the Personnel Section, every conversation of any kind with any other Soviet person called for lies. And if your idiot interlocutor said to you face to face that the Colorado beetles had been dropped on us by the Americans—it was necessary to agree! (And a shake of the head instead of a nod might well cost you resettlement in the Archipelago.)

But that was not all: Your children were growing up! And if the children were still little, then you had to decide what was the best way to bring them up; whether to start them off on lies instead of the truth (so that it would be *easier* for them to live) and then to lie forevermore in front of them too; or to tell them the truth, with the risk that they might make a slip, that they might let it out, which meant that you had to instill into them from the start that the truth was murderous, that beyond the threshold of the house you had to lie, only lie, just like papa and mama.

The choice was really such that you would rather not have any children.[57]

A society that is headed in the wrong direction can only be saved by the truth. The truth shines a light on our errors, which then allows us to make changes and improve. But without the truth, there can be no course correction when we are going the wrong way. And without a course correction, we will inevitably veer off the road and crash. If the individuals within a society sacrifice truth for comfort, then it appears there can only be one outcome—misery, death, and destruction.

Truth is the mechanism that keeps a society functioning. And the truth can only be told by an individual. The truth can only be told by *you*. This means we are stuck with a moral responsibility whether we like it or not. If we lie, we not only destroy ourselves, but we also destroy the world around us. And this observation is what led Solzhenitsyn to conclude that an individual who stopped lying could bring down a tyranny.[58]

It's easy to roll our eyes at this idea because we don't think what we do really matters. There's currently more than seven billion people in the world, how could one person's behavior make any sort of difference? This idea seems crazy until we begin to realize that we are not as disconnected from everyone as we originally thought. In fact, it appears that we are more like nodes in a network.[59] Let's say you interact with one thousand people in your lifetime, and all of those people also interact with one thousand people. That means you are only one person away from one million people, and two people away from one billion people—which means we are only a couple of connections away from everyone in the world! Who really knows how deeply our behavior can affect those around us, let alone the course of the world. Our actions may ripple out into the world like a stone thrown into a pond. How we act affects our family, what our family does affects the community, what our community does affects the state, etc. It's a bold claim, yet there may be some truth to it. How we live as individuals may impact the direction of humanity more than we ever thought was possible. Aleksandr Solzhenitsyn certainly seemed to think so.

The existentialists believe the only way to avoid hell is through the reduction of deceit.[60] They believe if we want to have a healthy and fulfilling life, we need to stop doing the things we know to be inadequate and wrong[61]—we need to stop lying to ourselves, we need to pay attention to the meanings we experience and allow these meanings to guide us, we need to respond to these meanings truthfully, no matter how unpleasant and uncomfortable it might be. And in doing so, we will become true *individuals*. We will become people who are strong enough to shoulder life's suffering. And we will have followed a path which will have given us a purpose so fulfilling that we find our suffering acceptable. Nietzsche writes:

> A traveler who had seen many countries and peoples and several continents was asked what human traits he had found everywhere; and he answered: men are inclined to laziness. Some will feel that he might have said with greater justice: they are all timorous. They hide behind customs and opinions. At bottom, every human being knows very well that he is in this world just once, as something unique, and that no accident, however strange, will throw together a second time into a unity such a curious and diffuse plurality: he knows it, but hides it like a bad conscience—why? From fear of his neighbor who insists on convention and veils himself with it.
>
> But what is it that compels the individual human being to fear his neighbor, to think and act herd-fashion, and not to be glad of himself? A sense of shame, perhaps, in a few rare cases. In the vast majority it is the desire for comfort, inertia—in short, that inclination to laziness of which the traveler spoke. He is right: men are even lazier than they are timorous, and what they fear most is the troubles with which an unconditional honestly and nudity would burden them.
>
> Only artists hate this slovenly life in borrowed manners and loosely fitting opinions and unveil the secret, everybody's bad conscience, the principle that every human being is a unique wonder; they dare to show us the human being as he is, down to the last muscle, himself and himself alone—even more, that in this rigorous consistency of his uniqueness he is beautiful and worth contemplating, as novel and incredible as every work of nature, and by no means dull.
>
> When a great thinker despises men, it is their laziness that he despises: for it is on account of this that they have

the appearance of factory products and seem indifferent and unworthy of companionship or instruction. The human being who does not wish to belong to the mass must merely cease being comfortable with himself; let him follow his conscience, which shouts at him: "Be yourself! What you are at present doing, opining, and desiring, that is not really you."[62]

## Recap

- Existentialism is an embodied philosophy—that is, it is a philosophy that requires you to act out what you believe.
- The lie destroys the individual and causes people to become resentful and seek revenge.
- The lie leads to the destruction of society.
- What we do matters. We are a node in a network. A single person can have a massive impact on the rest of the world.
- The meanings we experience are meant to inform us and guide us through life.
- The existentialists believe that we have a responsibility to pay attention to the meanings we experience, and to respond to these meanings truthfully—to do what we know to be right and to stop doing what we know to be wrong—that is, we have a responsibility to become true individuals. By doing so, we will avoid hell and become strong enough to face our suffering.

# CHAPTER SIX

## Morality

IF GOD IS DEAD, THEN who decides what is right and wrong? If not God, then that must mean people do. As soon as God was pronounced dead, we looked around the world and saw that cultures had different moralities; what one culture deemed to be wrong, another culture celebrated. Because of this, we began thinking about morality as a social construct—some arbitrary set of rules forced on us by the people in charge so that they could stay in power. And this line of reasoning eventually led to a belief in moral relativism, the idea that there is no ultimate right or wrong, and so, therefore, every individual can choose what is right or wrong for him- or herself.

Moral relativism is a problem. If there is no such thing as right and wrong, then that means we can do whatever we want. Truth will be decided by those who can hit first and hit the hardest. This kind of thinking will eventually lead the world into chaos. Which begs the question: is there another way forward or are we stuck with the consequences that are inevitably coming down the pike?

### The Games We Play

Although a logical case can be made for moral relativism, there is something about it that just feels wrong. In his book *The Gulag Archipelago*, Aleksandr Solzhenitsyn believed one of the most important events of the twentieth century was the Nuremberg trials because they concluded there are some behaviors that are universally wrong.[63]

These trials decided that the behaviors that characterized the Nazi atrocities in World War II were so horrific that the proper visceral embodied response of anyone observing—regardless of their culture or specific moral code—should be repugnance.[64]

> **"Genocide is a crime against humanity. No matter what the particulars of your moral code, so goes the logic, you cannot construct a viable moral code that enables genocide. If not a logical impossibility—and I think it is a logical impossibility—it's an ethical impossibility. And then you have to ask yourself—and this is not precisely an intellectual question—does that seem credible to you? Does it seem credible that there are acts that are so terrible that no one, regardless of their stated position, should ever engage in them?"[65]**

And if the answer to this question is "yes," while we may not have identified what is right, we most certainly have identified something that is wrong. And by identifying something that is wrong, we have taken our first step towards establishing a universal morality.[66]

Earlier we discussed Jean Piaget's theory of embodied cognition—the idea that we can embody more information than we consciously know. Now one of Piaget's goals was to bridge the gap between science and religion—that is basically why he did everything that he did.[67] And by studying the cognitive development of children, Piaget found—and this might be his most profound discovery—that morality naturally emerges out of the games we play with one another.[68]

Imagine playing a game. When we play games there are rules—things we are allowed to do and things we are not allowed to do—and those rules can be thought of as the morality of those games. Now according to Piaget, as humans began interacting and playing games with each other, we developed rules for the human game. And once the rules were established, if we didn't play by those rules, people would not want to play with us anymore.

Neuroscientist and psychologist Jaak Panksepp conducted an experiment with rats that highlighted this very phenomenon.[69] Rats like to wrestle. If Rat A is only 10 percent bigger than Rat B, then Rat A can pin Rat B virtually every time they play. Once Rat B loses, it is his job to invite Rat A to play again. What Panksepp discovered was that if Rat A doesn't let Rat B win at least 30 percent of the time, then Rat B won't invite Rat A to play anymore. Which shows how a morality—how we should behave—naturally emerges out of the games we play with one another.[70]

Because children like to play games, they have to play in a way that satisfies everyone involved, otherwise the game will end and no one will get to play. Therefore, as children play, they learn the proper way to act and will change their behavior depending on how the people around them are responding. In the same way, our species learned which behaviors were acceptable and which ones were not by interacting with the people around us:

> If you begin to deviate from the straight and narrow path—if you begin to act improperly—people will react to your errors before they become too great, and cajole, laugh, tap, and criticize you back into place. They will raise an eyebrow, or smile (or not), or pay attention (or not). If other people can tolerate having you around, in other words, they will constantly remind you not to misbehave, and just as constantly call on you to be at your best.[71]

How we play the game matters. If we play in a way that destroys the game, then that method of playing can be considered wrong. If everyone is playing basketball, and we decide to play football, the game will be over and everyone loses. This is what parents mean when they say things like "It doesn't matter if you win or lose, it's how you play the game."[72] Life is not one single game, it is a set of games, and we want to play those games in a way so that people will keep inviting us back to play for the rest of our lives. We are not successful if we only win one game, we are successful by being invited to play as many games as possible. Which means we must play fairly, even if there is a victory at stake.[73]

When we play in a way that satisfies our needs, as well as the needs of others simultaneously, we create a game that runs smoothly. Piaget referred to this kind of self-sustaining game as an *equilibrated* state, and believed it was not only the most productive game to play but also the most efficient. This is because if we play in a way that does not compliment the people around us, we waste a large amount of time and energy on conflict, which then results in a game that requires more work to maintain. This is why Piaget believed an equilibrated state would *always* outperform a disequilibrated state and, therefore, was a better game to play.[74]

If we want the games we play to be successful—meaning these games do not deteriorate and fall apart—then there are only a few ways we can actually play them. This is where moral relativism falls apart. Moral relativists claim that there are an unlimited amount of ways to interpret the world, which is correct. But then they go on to say, "And every interpretation of the world is equally valid." This could not be further from the truth. What the moral relativists fail to realize is that although there are an unlimited amount of games we can play, *not all games are equally playable*. Morality cannot be anything we want it to be because there are only a handful of ways we can act that will actually satisfy the needs of everyone involved. The majority of ways we could play a game are not efficient and would eventually cause the game to fall apart. If we are interested in creating a game where people can live together in a productive and harmonious way, we will find that there are many ways to interpret that problem, yet only a few solutions that actually work to solve it.

Once our species started interacting with each other, the rules for the human game began to emerge. We learned through trial and error which behaviors resulted in successful games, and which ones did not. And because there are not many ways to successfully play the human game, all cultures have an ethic that is fairly similar. It has to be that way, otherwise these cultures would not have lasted. Although moral codes can be different in the particulars, the underlying ethic does not have much room for variation. It's like asking whether or not languages are the same or different. The answer is they are both the same *and* different. Languages are clearly different in many ways, but they are also the same in terms of their underlying structure and foundation.[75]

A wolf pack knows how to live together—they know how to hunt together, raise pups together, and they know the social status of every wolf in their pack. In a sense, it's like wolves live according to a set of unspoken rules. Like all social animals, we too have rules for living together, rules which have been built into our behavior through hundreds of thousands of years of shared games. And like wolves, although we are not always conscious of these rules, we can feel when they are being violated.[76]

We have a nature, but because we are still in the process of discovering who we are as a species, that nature isn't always clear to us. Piaget believed that we acted in the world first, and as we evolved, we watched ourselves act and told stories about how we were acting. This means that the unconscious wisdom of mankind—our nature, our morality, our purpose—has been encoded into the ancient stories of our species. And if these stories contain such an ancient and profound wisdom, then perhaps they can provide us with an answer to the problem we are trying to solve.

> We're still chimps in a troupe, or wolves in a pack. We know how to behave. We know who's who, and why. We've learned that through experience. Our knowledge has been shaped by our interaction with others. We've established predictable routines and patterns of behavior—but we don't really understand them or know where they originated. They've evolved over great expanses of time. No one was formulating them explicitly (at least not in the dimmest reaches of the past), even though we've been telling each other how to act forever. One day, however, not so long ago, we woke up. We were already doing, but we started *noticing* what we were doing. We started using our bodies as devices to represent their own actions. We started imitating and dramatizing. We invented ritual. We started acting out our own experiences. Then we started to tell stories. We coded our observations of our drama in these stories. In this manner, the information that was first only embedded in our behavior become represented in our stories. But we didn't and still don't understand what it all means.[77]

## Recap

- Morality naturally emerges out of the games we play with one another.
- Not all games are equally playable. There are a limited number of

ways to successfully play the human game and, therefore, in the final analysis, morality cannot be relative.

- Humans watched the games they were playing and began to tell stories about those games.

- This means the ancient stories of mankind contain the unconscious wisdom of our species and, therefore, might be able to provide us with an answer to the problem we are trying to solve.

# Part One Recap

## Piaget and Embodied Cognition

As a species, we acted in the world first and then built ourselves from the bottom-up. We watched ourselves act and told stories about how we were acting. Because ancient stories are based on our behavior, they contain the pragmatic wisdom of our species, wisdom that we have yet to fully understand on a conscious level.

## Phenomenology

Ideas are tools that help us navigate the world. Every idea is based on a set of assumptions. If we change our assumptions about what it means for something to be "real," then we will find that the meanings we experience in life might be the most real thing we will ever come into contact with. Something does not need to have a physical/material/objective nature for it to be "real." The world of meaning—the world that we experience—is real, and it is our primary reality; it is a place that exists outside of the material world.

## Carl Rogers

Lies cause unnecessary suffering, and the truth is curative. We have an instinct that informs us when we are not being authentic to ourselves—that is, when we are doing or saying things we know are wrong. Carl Rogers believed that if we paid attention and allowed this instinct to guide us through life, then we would become congruent and reach our full potential as humans.

## Existentialism

Existentialism is an embodied philosophy; it is a philosophy that requires you to act out what you believe. The existentialists claim that when we lie we not only destroy ourselves, but we also destroy the world around us. They believe that in order to avoid hell we must pay attention to the meanings we experience and respond to these meanings as truthfully as possible; that in order to improve our lives we should do the things we know to be right and stop doing the things we know to be wrong. Embody the truth and avoid the lie—according to an existentialist, this is the way to become a true individual, and ultimately save the world from destruction.

## Morality

The morality of our species naturally emerges out of the games we play with one another. Because not all games are equally playable, there are a limited number of ways we can successfully play the human game. This means that although there may be some variation in the particulars, in the final analysis, morality—right and wrong—cannot be relative. The wisdom of our species—our nature, our morality, our purpose—can be found within the ancient stories of mankind. And if these stories contain such an ancient and profound wisdom, then perhaps they can provide us with an answer to the problem we are trying to solve.

# *Part Two*

# CHAPTER SEVEN

# The Foundation of Mythology

PEOPLE TYPICALLY THINK THAT MYTHOLOGY was written as an attempt to describe the scientific world, but this could not be further from the truth. These ancient stories could not have possibly been meant to describe the scientific world because the people who wrote them weren't scientists! In fact, it wouldn't have even crossed the minds of those who wrote mythology to describe the world scientifically because science was not even a thing until about five hundred years ago, roughly speaking.[78]

The people who wrote mythology didn't care about what objects were made out of, they cared about surviving. And in order to survive, we don't need to know what things are made of, we need to know what things *mean*—which is to say, we need to know how we should act. If we want to survive in the world, our primary concern should be whether or not something is going to hurt us, help us, or kill us. Which explains why when we look at the world we don't see objects first, we see meaning. Therefore—and this cannot be overstated— when our ancestors told stories, they weren't telling scientific stories about the world of objects, they were telling stories about *how we should act* in the world of meaning.[79]

## The Maps We Make

Humans are Point A to Point B creatures. And in order to get from Point A to Point B, we have to create a map of the world, otherwise we won't know where we are or where we are going. (**See Fig. 7.1 for a representation of a Point A to Point B map.**)[80]

As we have previously discussed, the world is simply too big for us to perceive everything all at once. In order for us to successfully create a map of the world, we first have to ignore almost everything— otherwise we would be completely flooded with information overload. But by ignoring almost everything, we are guaranteeing that we will eventually miss something important . . . sound familiar?

There is a famous experiment conducted by psychologist Daniel Simons that illustrates this idea beautifully.[81] The experiment begins with a video of two teams playing a game—team one has three players who are wearing white, and team two has three players who are wearing black. Each team has a basketball. The goal of the experiment is for you, the observer, to count the number of times the white team passes their basketball. Simple enough. The timer starts and both teams begin weaving in and out of each other while passing their basketballs around. And as they play their game, you stay focused on counting how many passes the white team makes. Eventually, the time runs out and you tell the experimenter how many times the white team passed their basketball. To which the experimenter responds, "That's right! Great job . . . And did you see the gorilla?" A what? He then rewinds the tape and sure enough, as you were counting, a large man dressed in a gorilla suit walks into center screen—right in the middle of everyone passing their basketballs—stands there for a couple of seconds beating his chest, and then slowly walks away.[82]

This experiment shows that what we value (counting basketballs) actually determines what we see and what we ignore![83] And because people value different things, it's entirely possible that the people who have different opinions than us actually see a completely different world. This is why it is important for us to listen to those who have different opinions. While we'd love to think that they are just spouting off nonsense, there is a good chance that they are actually screaming, "Look out for the gorilla!"

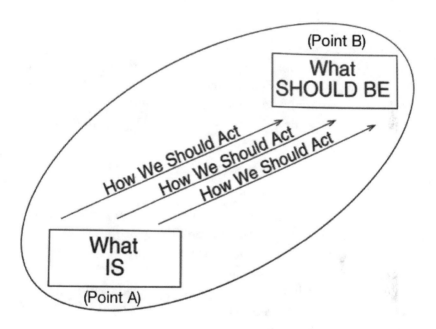

Figure 7.1

Now, again, in order to perceive anything, we have to ignore almost everything. And when we ignore almost everything, we are bound to miss something important—like a gorilla. And once we learn about a gorilla, it's up to us to incorporate this new piece of information into our existing map of the world—or we may even want to create a whole new map depending on the size of the gorilla. In a nutshell, this is what it means to be human. To be human means to strive for Point B, to fall, to learn something from that fall, to rise back up wiser and with a better map, and then to continue on towards Point B.

As humans, we cannot live without a map of the world. And it is our maps, these vital Point A to Point B structures, that cause three fundamental elements of human experience to emerge: *explored territory, unexplored territory, and the experiencer.*

## I. Explored Territory

When we first come across the term *explored territory* we usually think about land that has been discovered by explorers. And although this isn't a bad start, the explored territory that we are referring to is not actually a physical place. Remember, we don't live in the world of objects, we live in the world of meaning. Therefore, the explored territory we are referring to is a place that exists primarily within that world of meaning—that is, *it is a place that we experience.*

Explored territory is where we are when our maps of the world are working correctly; it is a place where everything goes according to plan and nothing unexpected happens.[84] Explored territory is *the known*, and it is the safety and security we feel when everything is behaving as it should be. But as soon as something unexpected happens, we realize that our maps are faulty and we no longer know where we are; and as a result, we leave the security of explored territory, and stumble into the much more unpredictable land of *unexplored territory*.

## II. Unexplored Territory

Unexplored territory is where we are when we don't know where we are. It is the land of *the unknown*, a place where unexpected things happen regularly.[85]

Like explored territory, unexplored territory exists within the world of meaning, which means it is a place that is not limited to a physical location. In fact, the same physical place can be explored territory in one moment and unexplored territory in the next.[86] For example, imagine that you are sitting in your living room and a snake suddenly slithers into the room—*a snake is an important difference between your living room one second ago and your living room now!*[87] Now, before the snake comes slithering into your living room, you are in one place—everything is going according to plan and you know where you are—but after the snake makes an appearance, you are somewhere completely different. In a split second your living room has transformed from a place that is familiar and safe, to a place that is dangerous and unpredictable.

Unexplored territory is where we are when the unexpected happens. It is where we find ourselves when we get fired from a job, lose a loved one, or discover we have been betrayed. It is home to the lost, scared, and confused; and once we enter into this domain, it can be a struggle to find our way out.

> **"When life falls apart, you don't get to ignore things anymore. You had this model of the world that told you what was relevant and what wasn't. And the real important part of that model was that it told you what *wasn't* relevant. Then all of a sudden, something pops up and takes you down— now *everything* is potentially relevant. And that's terribly stressful because everything is: Should I be angry? Should I be upset? Should I cry? Should I get divorced? Should I run away? Should I commit suicide? How am I going to come up with a new plan? Where am I going to get money? Who's going to help me? What's my future going to look like? What does my past look like? What am I going to do today? What am I going to do tomorrow?"[88]**

When we fall into unexplored territory, we no longer know where we are or what things mean. When we don't know what things mean, we don't know what to do. And when we don't know what to do, we freeze and prepare to do everything (commonly known as our fight or flight response). This is because an unexpected event could potentially mean anything, which means there is a chance that it could be the worst possible thing imaginable and, therefore, we have to be ready for that. As a result, encountering unexplored territory can be incredibly terrifying and stressful.[89]

But if an unexpected event can mean anything, then that also means it could mean the best possible thing imaginable as well. So when we enter into unexplored territory, we not only experience negative emotion, but we also might experience positive emotion simultaneously. Getting fired from a job might mean we are going to be homeless, but it also might mean we have a chance to find our dream job. Likewise, discovering that a significant other has been unfaithful might mean we are incapable of being loved, but it also might mean that we have an opportunity to stand up for ourselves and find a better companion and ultimately improve the quality of our lives.[90]

Explored and unexplored territory are so fundamental to the human experience that it appears in order to survive, our brains have actually evolved to help us navigate these two territories. The brain is divided into a right and left hemisphere, and each hemisphere serves a different function. The left hemisphere deals with the familiar and predictable world, while the right hemisphere deals with novelty.[91] In other words, the left hemisphere operates in explored territory,[92] and the right hemisphere operates in unexplored territory.[93] Now, if evolution is defined as "the body adapting to reality," and if our brains have evolved to represent explored and unexplored territory, then that means these two conceptual places can be considered a fundamental reality.[94]

Explored and unexplored territory are real places, they just don't exist in the physical world; they exist in a conceptual world—that is, in the world of meaning. *And to realize this is to realize that there is a reality that exists outside of the material world.*

## III. The Experiencer

The third fundamental element of human experience is *you*, the experiencer; the individual who turns unexplored territory into explored territory by facing the unknown, learning something new, and incorporating what they have learned into their map of the world. And it is this incorporation of new information into a faulty map that then allows the individual to rise back up into explored territory and continue on towards Point B.

These three fundamental realties—explored territory, unexplored territory, and the experiencer—are typically represented in mythology as dramatic characters so that we can better understand them. But before discussing these characters and how they developed, it may be helpful to first go over how our brains lend themselves to the creation of such characters.

## The Archetype

We started off as animals acting in the world, and as we evolved, we began to watch how we were acting. Once we began to observe the world around us, we started to recognize consistent *patterns*—not only patterns of behavior but also patterns relating to the structure of existence itself. And once we began seeing these patterns, we started to think about them. But the catch was that we couldn't think about these patterns in words because words were not a thing yet. Being able to consciously articulate our thoughts did not happen over night; that is, we didn't just wake up one day with the ability to think and speak in words—that was a skill that had to be developed over a very long period of time. And so when we started to think about these patterns, we had to think about them in a different way.

There are a lot of things that we know but cannot articulate with words. For example, we have a hard time articulating embodied knowledge—things like how to smile, how to whistle, or how to have a successful relationship.[95] Instead of thinking about these things in words, it would be more accurate to say that we think about them in images. For example, if I tell you to think about whistling, you will play a movie in your head of someone whistling. And it's only after we have pictured someone whistling in our minds, that we can begin to describe it using words. And because of this realization, both Jean Piaget and psychoanalyst Carl Jung believed that images and fantasy are what bridged the gap between our embodied knowledge and our conscious articulation[96]—that is, images and fantasy are what bridged the gap between our conscious and unconscious minds.

We think about things in images before we think about them in words because images are the natural language of the mind. The truth is that we don't really know how long our species has been using words, but the rough estimates range between one hundred fifty thousand years and two million years. Now, that length of time compared to however long our minds have been functioning without words—which some people estimate to be around *five hundred million years*—is an incredibly small amount of time. Our minds have been functioning without language for much longer than they have been functioning with language, and during that time, we had to be doing *something* to represent the world in a way that was prelinguistic.[97]

And so, as our species played the human game, we began to notice patterns in the world. And once we saw these patterns, we began to think about them in images. And it was these same fundamental patterns that we saw in the world and represented in images that Carl Jung referred to as *archetypes*.

**"There are all sorts of things that are universal about human beings . . . Imagine you have an instinct like anger . . . If you wanted to represent anger, maybe you would represent it like a drama; like a story. That's actually what you want to know if someone gets angry, right—what happened? Now imagine that you took one thousand stories about angry people and boiled them all into one story so everything that was common about anger was encapsulated into one single story. Well that would be the archetypal story of anger. And everyone would recognize it because it's anger represented in its purest form. *That's an archetype.*"[98]**

An archetype is a fundamental pattern of existence that is universally understood by all people. And the ability to recognize and understand these archetypes—these fundamental patterns of existence—is rooted *deep* within our unconscious minds. That's why when we come into contact with an archetype, even if we do not consciously understand it, we are immediately gripped by it.

"You remember in *Pinocchio* that Pinocchio's father is stuck in a whale, and Pinocchio has to go down there and rescue him.[99] It turns out you have to go to the bottom of the ocean and find your father in a whale, and then drown—that's how you stop being a puppet. You think you don't believe that, but I would say, yes you do! You went and watched the movie, and you enjoyed it. Not only that, but you understood it even though you don't have any idea what it's about. On the face of it, it's absolutely absurd! First of all, it's not a puppet, it's a drawing of a puppet—so that's two levels of weird. And what the hell is with the cricket? Where'd he come from? And what's his role? And why is he the conscience? And why does he get activated by a fairy? And why is the fairy a star? You're in there like Cletus the Slack-Jawed Yokel watching the screen captivated by it, and then you walk out and don't even notice that you're so peculiar that it's just beyond belief! It's like, *what the hell are you doing in that theater watching this marionette follow a bug around to a whale?!*[100] You don't even know how his father got in the whale. The last time you see his father he was in a rainstorm and then the next thing that happens is he's in a whale. And you're sitting there thinking, 'Hey, no problem. This all makes sense.' It's like . . . What? Really?! Why? How does that make sense?[101] Why would any of that happen? And the answer is, *you know why but you can't say why.* You can't say what it is that you know but the mere fact that it makes sense—and it does—is an indication from a Jungian perspective that you're operating at an archetypal level."[102]

Archetypes are patterns that our unconscious minds have consistently observed in the world. And once observed, we then represent these patterns in symbolic images. Now, when our ancestors began to tell stories about these patterns, they would use these symbolic images in their stories because they had no other way of expressing the patterns that they were seeing. Which means that the unconscious archetypal image—the fantasy or *the dream*—is the foundation for all mythology.[103]

Our ancestors were not stupid, they just looked at the world through a different lens. Mythology describes the world that we experience—a place to act, as opposed to a place of things. And although mythology may be scientifically and historically inaccurate, it is still true—it is just true in a different way. These ancient stories describe patterns that *really* exist in the world, and something that describes the fundamental patterns of human existence might be the most accurate description of the world that we have ever come up with.

> **"We know that what Shakespeare wrote is fiction. Then we say, 'Fiction isn't true.' But then you think, 'Well, wait a minute. Maybe it's true like numbers are true.' Numbers are an abstraction from the underlying reality, but no one in their right mind would really think that numbers aren't true. You could even make a case that the numbers are more real than the things that they represent because that abstraction is so insanely powerful. Once you have mathematics, you're just deadly. You can move the world with mathematics. It's not obvious that the abstraction is less real than the more concrete reality. You take a work of fiction like Hamlet and you think, 'It's not true, because it's fiction.' But what kind of explanation is that? Maybe it's *more true* than nonfiction [because it takes many stories about people, and abstracts out what they all have in common], and then it says, 'Here's something that's a key part of the human experience.'"[104]**

## How We Categorize

We cannot fully appreciate mythology without at least some understanding of how we categorize the world. Humans observe patterns in the world and represent those patterns in image. And the form these images take are partly determined by how our brains naturally categorize things.

For a long time, the academic world believed that humans categorized based on something called a *proper set*. An object that belongs to a proper set has the same characteristics of everything within that set, and no characteristics of anything outside of that set. Take a triangle, for example. A triangle is a closed three-sided figure. Regardless of its size or degree of its angles, a triangle will always be a triangle. Period. And what allows something to be considered a part of the "triangle proper set" is whether or not it is a closed three-sided figure; the rules of a proper set state that something is either a triangle or it is not.[105]

But humans do not naturally categorize the world using the proper set model. In fact, categorizing the world this way is actually a lot harder than it appears:

> People are very good at categorizing—so good, in fact, that the ability is taken for granted and appears simple. It is not so simple, however. Neither the "rules" that underly categorization, nor the act in itself, have proved easy to describe. Roger Brown, the eminent psycholinguist, states:

>> "In retrospect, it is amazing that psychology was for so long able to think of real-life categories as proper sets. We ought to have worried more over the extreme difficulty everyone has in defining anything "natural," and natural, as used here, includes not only dogs and carrots but also artifacts like chairs, cars, and pencils. I know you can tell one when you see one, but just try listing the attributes that are true of all dogs and of no cats or wolves or hyenas, or of all the carrots and no radishes or turnips, or of all chairs and no small tables, hassocks, benches or slings."[106]

We know that dogs are not cats, wolves, or hyenas; that carrots are not radishes or turnips; and that chairs are not small tables, hassocks, or benches; but we struggle to explain how we know these things belong to different categories. This is because humans have a very sophisticated way of categorizing the world—a method of categorization that is referred to as the *cognitive model*.[107]

The cognitive model of categorization is based on a distinct number of properties:

1) Two things may be placed within the same category if they evoke the same behavior.

> To say that two separate things belong to the same category is a tricky business. We presume, without thinking, that we group things as a consequence of something about them, rather than as a consequence of something about us. What do all *chairs* share in common, then? Any given chair may lack some of the most common chair attributes, such as legs, backs, or armrests. Is a tree-stump a chair? Yes, if you can sit on it. It isn't really something about an object, considered as an independent thing, that makes it a chair: it is, rather, something about its potential for interaction with us.[108]

2) Because things that evoke the same behavior can be placed within the same category, they can also be regarded as the same thing. For example, everything that belongs to the category of *things that you should run away from in terror*, whether that be a tiger or a crazy ex-lover, are actually the same thing—that is, something from which you should run away from in terror! And since everything within a category can be treated as the same, anything within that category can symbolically represent the entire category as a whole.

3) Things are usually remembered and categorized by their most memorable and understandable qualities. For instance, flowers may belong to the category of *things that you smell*, dogs may belong to the category of *things that you pet*, and tigers, as well as crazy ex-lovers, may belong to the category of *things that you run away from in terror*.

4) Things within a single category have something called *membership gradience*.

> Membership gradience implies degree of membership, which is to say that an ostrich, for example, is a bird, but perhaps not so much of a bird as a robin—because the robin has more properties, that are *central* to the category *bird*. A thing can

be a better or worse exemplar of its category; if it is worse, it can still be placed within that category.[109]

5) "They contain phenomena associated as a consequence of *familial resemblance*, a term used first in this context by Ludwig Wittgenstein."[110]

> Things with familial resemblance all share similarities with a potentially hypothetical object. The prototypical Smith brother, to use a famous example, may have a dark mustache, beady eyes, balding pate, thick horned rimmed glasses, dark beard, skinny neck, large ears and weak chin. Perhaps there are six Smith brothers, in total, none of whom has all the properties of the prototypical Smith. Morgan Smith has a weak chin, large ears, balding pate and skinny neck—but no glasses, mustache, or beard. Terry, by contrast, has the glasses, mustache and beard—but a full head of hair, small ears and a normal neck. Nelson has a receding hairline, beady eyes, and a dark beard and mustache—and so on for Lance, Randy and Lyle. None of the brothers precisely resembles another, but if you saw them in a group, you would say, "those men are all related."[111]

At the end of the day, the point being made is: the way in which we categorize the world has determined what images we use to represent the fundamental patterns of existence. And it is these unconscious images that serve as the foundation of mythology.

Mythology takes the archetypal patterns that we think about imagistically and portrays them as characters in a story. And if we want to truly understand these ancient stories, we must first become more familiar with who these archetypal characters are and how exactly they emerged.

## Recap

- Ancient stories are not scientific descriptions of the world, they are stories about how we should act.
- The three fundamental elements of human experience are explored territory, unexplored territory, and the experiencer.

- Explored territory (the known) is the conceptual place you inhabit when everything is going according to plan. It is where you are when you know where you are.
- Unexplored territory (the unknown) is the conceptual place you inhabit when the unexpected happens. It is where you are when you do not know where you are.
- Our brains have evolved to operate within explored and unexplored territory. If evolution is defined as "the body adapting to reality," and if our brains have evolved to represent explored and unexplored territory, then that means these two conceptual places should be considered a fundamental reality. *To realize this is to realize that there is a reality that exists outside of the material world.*
- Image—fantasy or the dream—works as a bridge between unconscious knowledge and conscious understanding.
- A fundamental pattern of existence is called an *archetype.*
- We observed archetypal patterns in the world and represented those patterns as dynamic images. These images were then later expressed as characters in a story.
- Our natural ability to categorize the world, alongside our inclination to represent archetypal patterns as images, is the foundation of all mythology.

CHAPTER EIGHT

# The Players of Mythology
# - Part One

*"All the world's a stage,*
*And all the men and women merely players:*
*They have their exits and their entrances;*
*And one man in his time plays many parts."*

— Shakespeare, *As You Like It*

IN THE BEGINNING OF *THE Lion King*, Mufasa and his son, Simba, sit at the top of Pride Rock and look out over the vast African plains. As they watch the sun rise, Mufasa informs Simba that everything the light touches is their kingdom. An impressed Simba then scans the horizon and asks, "And what about that shadowy place?" "That's beyond our borders," Mufasa answers, "you must never go there, Simba."

Explored territory exists everywhere the light touches. *It is our kingdom.* And beyond its borders is the unknown—a shadowy place full of terrifying things. Now, because explored and unexplored territory are so fundamental to the human experience, we will also find that they are essential for understanding the mythological landscape.

Explored and unexplored territory are represented in mythology as *chaos and order.* When we are in explored territory, we experience order. Order is structure, routine, and the sense of security we feel when everything is going according to plan. It is everything that lies within the castle walls, and that which protects us from the unknown. Order is Hogwarts in *Harry Potter*, the Shire in *The Lord of the Rings*, and Gepetto's workshop in *Pinocchio*. For all intents and purposes, order is the security and predictability we feel when positioned safely behind the walls of culture.

> Order . . . is *explored territory*. That's the hundreds-of-millions-of-years-old hierarchy of place, position and authority. That's the structure of society... Order is tribe, religion, hearth, home and country. It's the warm, secure living-room where the fireplace glows and the children play. It's the flag of the nation. It's the value of the currency. Order is the floor beneath your feet, and your plan for the day. It's the greatness of tradition, the rows of desks in a school classroom, the trains that leave on time, the calendar, and the clock. Order is the public facade we're called upon to wear, the politeness of a gathering of civilized strangers, and the thin ice on which we all skate. Order is the place where the behavior of the world matches our expectations and our desires; the place where all things turn out the way we want them to. . . .[112]
> Order is the peacetime army of policemen and soldiers. It's the political culture, the corporate environment, and the system. It's the "they" in "you know what they say." It's credit cards, classrooms, supermarket checkout lineups, turn taking, traffic lights, and the familiar routes of daily commuters.[113]

And when we stumble from explored territory into unexplored territory, we experience chaos. Chaos is everything that exists outside of order. It is nature—that which surrounds the protective walls of culture and tries to break through. It is the barbarians at the gates, the dark enchanted forest, and Alice down the rabbit hole. Chaos is what we experience when we no longer know where we are or what we should do. It is the elephant graveyard and a home to lost souls.

> Chaos is the domain of ignorance itself. It's *unexplored territory*. Chaos is what extends, eternally and without limit, beyond

the boundaries of all states, all ideas, and all disciplines. It's the foreigner, the stranger, the member of another gang, the rustle in the bushes in the night-time, the monster under the bed, the hidden anger of your mother, and the sickness of your child. Chaos is the despair and horror you feel when you have been profoundly betrayed. It's the place you end up when things fall apart; when your dreams die, your career collapses, or your marriage ends.[114]

When we enter into unexplored territory, we come into contact with chaos; a journey that is symbolically represented in mythology as *a descent into the underworld*.[115] And once we understand that a journey to the underworld is the same thing as entering into unexplored territory, we have one of the keys necessary for understanding mythology. And if we can understand mythology, then we might be able to uncover some of the wisdom encoded in these stories.[116]

## The Landscape of Mythology

Human experience has a very specific structure, and mythology represents that structure in a very specific way. The landscape of mythology goes something like this: the individual exists within explored territory and is surrounded by unexplored territory; or the individual is protected by the walls of culture and is surrounded by nature; or the individual is protected by order and is surrounded by chaos. And according to mythology, these three elements—the individual, chaos, and order—all arise out of an infinite field of potential which we will refer to as *the precosmogonic chaos*.

The diagram presented in **Fig. 8.1** portrays the landscape of mythology, a landscape containing the totality of human experience—that is, a landscape that tells the whole story of mankind. Now, if something is a totality, that means it has both beneficial and destructive characteristics. Take order, for example; order is what gives us direction and protects us from the terrifying unknown. But too much order can also suffocate. Likewise, chaos is the source of all new things, which means it is not only the source of those things that nourish, revitalize, and help us grow, but it is also the source of those things that produce catastrophe and despair. And lastly, the individual is not only the helping hand, the best friend, and the soulmate, but he is also the liar, the thief, and the dagger in the back.

Humans are incredibly social creatures, which means our environment isn't so much the objective world, as much as it is the people around us. Where we are and how we should act largely depends on other people—who they are, who they are attached to, and how they are behaving. For example, if you are in a restaurant having a nice dinner and someone pulls out a gun, that will drastically change the environment you are in (where you are and how you should behave). Likewise, if you are being pursued by an attractive woman, whether you are in a dangerous environment or a safe environment does not depend on the objective world, but rather, on whether this woman is single or the intoxicated wife of a large, dangerous man.[117] Therefore, because the people around us determine where we are and how we should behave, our brains have evolved specifically to understand our social environment first and foremost. And it is for this reason that we naturally perceive the world through a social lens.[118]

Our tendency to view the world through a social lens causes us to see the world as if it is personified. This is the reason why cars look like they have faces; the reason why inanimate objects are alive in children's books;[119] and the reason why we cry when Tom Hanks loses his best friend, Wilson, *a volleyball*, in the iconic movie *Castaway*. And because humans naturally see the world as if it is personified, our ancestors experienced the fundamental elements of human experience—explored territory, unexplored territory, the individual, and the precosmogonic chaos—as *personalities* and, therefore, placed them into the social categories that our brains had already developed: categories such as *male and female*, but even more specifically, *mother* and *father*.

Thus, the category of "parent" and/or "child" has been around for 200 million years. That's longer than birds have existed. That's longer than flowers have grown. It's not a billion years, but it's still a very long time. It's plenty long enough for male and female and parent and child to serve as vital and fundamental parts of the environment to which we have adapted.

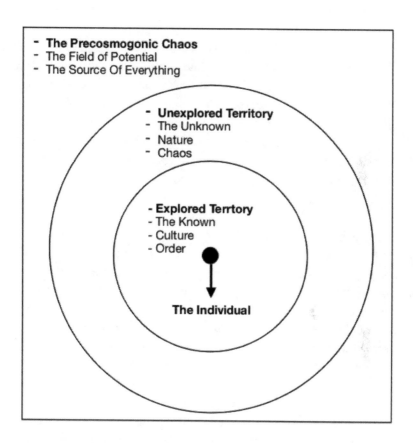

- **The Precosmogonic Chaos**
- The Field of Potential
- The Source Of Everything

- **Unexplored Territory**
- The Unknown
- Nature
- Chaos

- **Explored Terrtory**
- The Known
- Culture
- Order

**The Individual**

Figure 8.1

This means that male and female and parent and child are categories, for us—natural categories, deeply embedded in our perceptual, emotional and motivational structures.[120]

Father, mother, and child—child being us, the individual—are three fundamental categories mankind has used to understand the world. But there is also a fourth category we use to understand the world that is just as ancient and important. And that is the category of *predator*. Therefore, the four basic categories that humans use to understand the world are *mother, father, the individual, and predator*. And it was out of these four categories that the characters of mythology were born.

## The Precosmogonic Chaos

The precosmogonic chaos is essentially a state of pure potential. For example, consider the future—when we think about the future, we feel that it is full of potential and possibility. And in a sense, it is this very potential that mythology represents as the precosmogonic chaos.[121] The precosmogonic chaos is the source of all things; it is the field of potential that everything materializes out of, and where things "exist" before they actually exist.

The precosmogonic chaos is the ultimate unknown. Think about it this way: there are things that we know we don't know, and then there are things we don't have any clue we don't know. The chaos we have been referring to up until this point is the unknown that we are aware of; the *known* unknown, so to speak—that is, the unknown that is directly related to explored territory. But the precosmogonic chaos is the *unknown* unknown; it is the category of things we cannot even conceptualize because we are completely unaware of their possibility. Known unknowns we can plan for; unknown unknowns are completely unimaginable and unexpected.[122]

The precosmogonic chaos contains all the unknown unknowns, all the things we cannot think up or anticipate. And although our ancestors could not imagine what these unknown things were, they still understood that they existed and, therefore, needed to represent them somehow. And the way our ancestors ended up representing the precosmogonic chaos—the field of potential that contains all unknown

Figure 8.2

Figure 8.3

unknowns—was with something called a *uroboros*; otherwise known as the *Dragon of Chaos* (see Fig. 8.2 and Fig. 8.3).[123]

Evolution is a conservative process.[124] And because it took millions of years to develop the brain structures that we currently have, it would make no sense to tear those structures down and start over from scratch. Therefore, as we continue to grow and evolve, it makes the most sense to use the structures that we already have in place as a foundation, and then build new structures on top of them.

Now, archaic man would have obviously experienced predators as threatening and dangerous. And as our ancestors evolved, they eventually developed the ability to think abstractly. Which means that instead of thinking about specific dangerous predators, they developed the ability to start thinking about danger as an abstract concept. And because we built upon the brain structures that were already in place, *the same system our ancient ancestors used to detect predators is the same system that we now use to detect all threatening and dangerous things.*[125]

"The system we used to identify and run away from things that ate us when we were thirty-pound mammals is the same system we now use to process relatively abstract threats. And why wouldn't it be? As far as I'm concerned, this isn't even a hypothesis. We know evolution is conservative; everything builds on what was there before. What else are you going to use when you're threatened by some abstract threat except the system that you used to use when you were threatened by a crocodile?"[126]

The unknown is a place that is full of danger, and therefore we experience it as if it were a predator. This is why when we come into contact with the unknown, our first impulse is to freeze like an animal trying to avoid the gaze of a vicious beast (think *Jurassic Park*). Ultimately, this explains why the precosmogonic chaos—the *ultimate* unknown—is represented in mythology as a dragon, the *ultimate* predator.

Representations of dragons are incredibly common across the world. Some believe the reason for this is because our tree-dwelling ancestors consistently battled three types of predators: cats, birds of prey, and our most ancient of enemies, snakes.[127] And so, when we experience the ultimate unknown, we actually represent it symbolically as a combination of these three common predators—which means a dragon is fundamentally a cat-snake-bird that breathes fire (fire being another thing belonging to the category of *threatening and dangerous things*).

Although we experience the precosmogonic chaos as something that is threatening and dangerous, it is also a totality, which means that it has a beneficial aspect as well. The ultimate unknown, although dangerous, can also contain helpful information; things we can learn from our encounter that will make us stronger. This kind of information is incredibly valuable because it helps us to build better maps of the world. Which is why in mythology the Dragon of Chaos is typically guarding something of value like gold or a young virgin.

The precosmogonic chaos is something like a predatory cat and/or reptile because it lurks in the unknown, waiting to devour us. It is something like a bird of prey because it can swoop down out of nowhere and take us by surprise. It is something like fire because it can destroy, but if harnessed correctly, can be transformative. It is something that has legs and wings because it lives in both the conceptual and material world.[128] The precosmogonic chaos is unmanifested potential. It is the source of *everything*: masculine and feminine, day and night, creation and destruction.

**"The reason it's got its tail in its mouth—the idea this thing is trying to represent—is that it is complete unto itself. So it's a symbol of totality. It's *everything*. How? Well, you walk into the room where your interview is, you might ask, 'What's in there?' A better question is, 'What's *not* in there?' That's a better question because your whole damn future's in there and you don't even know how much that branches out. Your future's there, the future of your children is in there, the future of your grandchildren is in there.[129] And that's what is symbolized by the Dragon of Chaos. That's why it's *multi-dimensional predator* plus *thing that holds treasure* at the**

same time. Here's a way of thinking about it: in order for us to guard ourselves properly against the absolute unknown, we had to conceptualize it first. I can say 'absolute unknown.' . . . That's such a strange category. It's the category of all things that have not yet been categorized. It's like the number zero. It took people a long time to come up with the idea of zero; it's the category that contains nothing. Well, what do you need a category like that for? *To do mathematics as it turns out!* The Dragon of Chaos is the category of all things that have not yet been mastered. And your job is to be a master of all things that have not yet been mastered. And you're not going to do that until you can conceptualize it. And so you conceptualize it with the gold-hoarding meta-predator.[130] Because we can only use the representational structures that we evolved, it's a paradoxical representation of the predator and the treasure that lies beyond the perimeters of our safe societies . . . It's the predator that lurks in the unknown and also harbors something of value. Perfect. That's exactly right."[131]

## The Great Father

Explored territory is represented in mythology as order. Order is what protects us from the terrifying unknown and transforms the world into a safer, more predictable place. Essentially, order is the walls of culture. And because the essence—or the spirit—of *that which builds walls and protects* is undeniably masculine, our ancestors associated order with men.

> Order, the known, appears symbolically associated with masculinity . . . This is perhaps because the primary hierarchical structure of human society is masculine, as it is among most animals, including the chimpanzees who are our closest genetic and, arguably, behavioral match. It is because men are and throughout history have been the builders of towns and cities, the engineers, stonemasons, bricklayers, and lumberjacks, the operators of heavy machinery.[132]

Historically speaking, men not only protect and provide for their families, but also for society as a whole. Men establish rules and enforce those rules so that society can function and have a chance to flourish. As a result, our ancestors placed order into the cognitive social category of *father*, which then caused them to represent order—explored territory—as the *Great Father* in mythology.

The Great Father is an archetype that represents the totality of order. And because order is a totality, it has both a beneficial and destructive aspect. Therefore, the Great Father is symbolically represented in mythology by two characters: the *Protective Father* and the *Tyrannical Father*.

## I. The Protective Father

Culture constrains the individual, there is no doubt about it. But some constraints are beneficial. For example, a lot of times when children are having fun they run around screaming at the top of their lungs, something that can be incredibly annoying and destructive. That being the case, the job of a parent is to socialize their children so that they can one day become productive members of society, a job which largely takes the form of discipline and constraint. Children who are not properly socialized have worse lives. Plain and simple. Which is why parents of young children are constantly yelling at them to behave.[133] Disciplining a child, while unpleasant, is extremely necessary for their overall growth and wellbeing.

Now discipline is a form of tyranny, and although discipline can be painful, it is also a prerequisite for success. For example, before we can become doctors or lawyers, we must first learn how to read, write, and speak properly, as well as learn how to sit quietly and pay attention in a classroom setting. And so, although it takes a tremendous amount of constraint and discipline to mold someone into a doctor or a lawyer, these constraints are what ultimately allow us to have better lives.

In mythology, this beneficial aspect of culture is represented by the Protective Father—the classic wise king or wise old man character. The Protective Father provides and protects. He disciplines his children so that they can become functioning members of society and, therefore, have a chance to succeed in life. He is the enforcer of rules, the teacher of sacred traditions, and a conduit of wisdom. It is his shoulders upon which we stand and think that we are flying.

> Every word we speak is a gift from our ancestors. Every thought we think was thought previously by someone smarter. The highly functional infrastructure that surrounds us, particularly in the West, is a gift from our ancestors: the comparatively uncorrupt political and economic systems, the technology, the wealth, the lifespan, the freedom, the luxury, and the opportunity. Culture takes with one hand, but in some fortunate places it gives more with the other. . . .[134]
>
> The wise king maintains stability, not because he is afraid of the unknown, but because nothing new can be built without a strong foundation . . . He is a house with doors; a structure that shelters, but does not stifle; a master who teaches and disciplines but does not indoctrinate or crush. He represents the tradition fostering cooperation among people whose shared culture makes trust possible, even easy . . . The monsters of chaos are locked up in his dungeon or banished to the nether regions of the kingdom. He is the personality of dead heroes (that is, the action patterns and hierarchies of value established through exploration in the past) organized according to the principle of "respect for the intrinsic value of the living." This makes him the king who takes advice from his subjects—who is willing to enter into creative interchange with those he "dominates" legally—and to benefit from this advice from the "unworthy."[135]

The Protective Father is Mufasa in *The Lion King*, the tender-hearted, fierce protector of the Pride Lands. He is Dumbledore in *Harry Potter*, the competent, good-humored headmaster of Hogwarts. He is Yoda in *Star Wars*, Mr. Miyagi in *The Karate Kid*, and Eddard Stark in *Game of Thrones*. Lastly, he is Gandalf from *The Lord of the Rings*, the wise, humble wizard who stands his ground against "a demon of the ancient world" in order to save his friends.

Order is what beneficially constrains the individual, but if we are not careful, this constraint can go too far. Although constraint is necessary for growth, too much constraint can suffocate. At some point, beneficial constraint can transform into a life-crushing force, and the desire to protect can morph into the desire to imprison. Here is where we meet the darker side of the Great Father, the negative aspect of culture that is represented in mythology by the *Tyrannical Father*.

## II. The Tyrannical Father

The rules of culture make everything predictable and therefore provide us with security. But if culture becomes too attached to this security, any deviation from the rules will be seen as a threat. The rules and traditions of our culture contain wisdom, but that does not mean they are infallible. Because we can never know absolute truth, there is always a chance we will come across new information that will make it necessary for us to update the old rules. But if culture, in the name of safety and security, refuses to update, then it will become too stagnant for the beneficial aspect to survive. And once this happens, all that will remain are the rules . . . or else.

Despite evidence that the current rules need an update, the tyrannical aspect of culture is too set in its ways to acknowledge the truth, and anyone who attempts to update these rules will be labeled as a heretic and swiftly removed from the picture. This is how the beneficial aspect of culture can become corrupted and turn into tyranny. And it is this destructive aspect of culture that is portrayed in mythology by the character of the Tyrannical Father.

> The conservative tendency of any culture, striving to maintain itself, can easily transform into the deadening weight of absolute authority. The Great Father as tyrant destroys what he once was and undermines what he still depends upon . . . This is the aspect of the Great Father that motivates adolescent rebellion and gives rise to ideological narratives attributing to society everything that produces the negative in man. It is the Tyrannical Father who consumes his own children, and who walls up the virgin princess in an inaccessible place. The

Tyrannical Father rules absolutely, while the kingdom withers or becomes paralyzed; his decrepitude and age are matched only by his arrogance, inflexibility and blindness to evil. He is the personification of the authoritarian or totalitarian state, whose "goal" is reduction of all who are currently living to manifestation of a single dead "past" personality.[136]

The Tyrannical Father is the enemy of possibility; he opposes anything new that threatens his authority or the status quo.[137] He denies the need for improvement while crushing those who suggest otherwise. The Tyrannical Father is Scar from *The Lion King*, Darth Vader from *Star Wars*, and Captain Hook in *Peter Pan*. He is *Aladdin's* Jafar, Saruman from *The Lord of the Rings*, and Judge Claude Frollo, the archdeacon of Notre Dame who keeps his "son" locked away from the world for his own good.

Culture suffocates and protects us simultaneously; we cannot have one without the other. Therefore, the Protective Father and the Tyrannical Father always exist at the same time, and together represent the totality of order.

## The Great Mother

Unexplored territory is represented in mythology as chaos. Chaos is the unknown; it is nature; it is everything that lies outside the walls of culture, and everything we do not understand.

Everything we currently know was once unknown to us and is a result of someone exploring something they did not understand. This means that all new things come out of the unknown. And because the unknown, like women, gives birth to new things, our ancestors associated the unknown with femininity,[138] and therefore placed chaos into the fundamental social category of *mother*.

The unknown appears to be generally conceptualized or symbolically represented as female primarily because the female genitalia—hidden, private, unexplored, productive—serve as "gateway" or "portal" to the "(divine) unknown world of source of creation," and therefore easily come to stand for that "place."

Novelty and femininity share analogical or categorical identity, from this perspective: both constitute a window, so to speak, into the world "beyond." Woman, insofar as she is subject to natural demands, is not merely a model for nature—she is divine nature, in imagination and actuality. She literally *embodies* the matrix of biological being . . . The matrix of all things is something *feminine*, like the mothers of experience; it is something with an endlessly fecund and renewed (maternal and virginal) nature—something that defines fertility and, therefore, femininity itself. Things come from somewhere; all things have their birthplace.[139]

In fact, this is why we refer to nature as *Mother* Nature. Nature gives birth to all life, and then nourishes that life.

The Mother of Songs, the mother of our whole seed, bore us in the beginning. She is the mother of all races of men and the mother of all tribes. She is the mother of the thunder, the mother of the rivers, the mother of trees and of all kinds of things. She is the mother of songs and dances. She is the mother of the older brother stones. She is the mother of the grain and the mother of all things. She is the mother of the younger brother Frenchmen and of the strangers. She is the mother of the dance paraphernalia and of all temples, and the only mother we have. She is the mother of the animals, the only one, and the mother of the Milky Way. It was the mother herself who began to baptize. She gave us the limestone coca dish. She is the mother of the rain, the only one we have. She alone is the mother of all things, she alone. And the mother has left a memory in all the temples. With her sons, the saviors, she left songs and dances as a reminder. Thus the priests, the fathers, and the older brothers have reported.[140]

For these reasons, among others, our ancestors represented chaos as the *Great Mother*. And the Great Mother, like the Great Father, is a totality, which means that she has both a beneficial and destructive aspect. Therefore, the Great Mother is symbolically represented in mythology by two characters: the *Creative Mother* and the *Destructive Mother*.

*"Are you a good witch, or a bad witch?"*
–Glinda, the Good Witch of the North

## I. The Creative Mother

The Creative Mother represents the beneficial aspect of the unknown and is responsible for all new things that are good. She is the miracle, the stroke of good luck, and divine intervention. She inspires hope, faith, and belief by offering signs when they are needed most. She is the epiphany and the eureka moment. She is the wisdom that saves and the information that transforms.

The Creative Mother is Glinda, the Good Witch of the North in *The Wizard of Oz*, who gives Dorothy hope and direction during her time of need. She is the Blue Fairy in *Pinocchio*, who not only gives Pinocchio life, but also miraculously saves him from trouble, teaches him important life lessons, and tells him where he can find his missing father. The Creative Mother is Cinderella's Fairy Godmother, the miracle who appears when Cinderella has lost all hope of attending the royal ball. And lastly, she is the Three Good Fairies in *Sleeping Beauty* who free Prince Phillip from his imprisonment and provide him with weapons to save Princess Aurora.

The Creative Mother represents all beneficial things that emerge from the unknown. But while the Great Mother gives with one hand, she mercilessly takes with the other.

## II. The Destructive Mother

In her beneficial guise, the Great Mother is the source of all good things; she is newly acquired wisdom, the giver of hope, and the wellspring of life. But in her destructive guise, however, the Great Mother is not so generous.

For this woman who generates life and all living things on earth is the same who takes them back into herself, who pursues her victims and captures them with snare and net. Disease, hunger, hardship, war above all, are her helpers, and among all peoples the goddesses of war and the hunt express man's experience of life as a female exacting blood. This Terrible Mother is the hungry earth, which devours its own children and fattens on their corpses; it is the tiger and the vulture, the vulture and the coffin, the flesh-eating sarcophagus voraciously licking up the wood seed of men and beasts and, once fecundated and sated, casting it out again in new birth, hurling it to death, and over and over again to death....[141]

The Great Mother, in her negative guise, is the force that induces the child to cry in the absence of her parents. She is the branches that claw at the night traveler, in the depths of the forest. She is the terrible force that motivates the commission of atrocity—planned rape and painful slaughter—during the waging of war. She is aggression, without the inhibition of fear and guilt; sexuality in the absence of responsibility, dominance without compassion, greed without empathy. She is the Freudian id, unconsciousness contaminated with the unknown and mortal terror, and the flies in the corpse of a kitten. She is everything that jumps in the night, that scratches and bites, that screeches and howls; she is paralyzing dismay, horror and the screams that accompany madness. The Great Mother aborts children, and is the dead fetus; breeds pestilence, and is the plague; she makes the skull something gruesomely compelling, and is all skulls herself. To unveil her is to risk madness, to gaze over the abyss, to lose the way, to remember the repressed trauma. She is the molester of children, the golem, the bogey-man, the monster in the swamp, the rotting cadaverous zombie who threatens the living. She is progenitor of the devil, the "strange son of chaos." She is the serpent, and Eve, the temptress; she is the *femme fatale,* the insect in the ointment, the hidden cancer, the chronic sickness, the plague of locusts, the cause of drought, the poisoned water. She uses erotic pleasure as a bait to keep the world alive and breeding; she is a gothic monster who feeds on the blood of the living. She is the water that washes menacingly over the ridge of the crumbling dam; the shark

in the depths, the wide-eyed creature of the deep forests, the
cry of the unknown animal, the claws of the grizzly and the
smile of the criminally insane. The Great and Terrible Mother
stars in every horror movie, every black comedy; she lies in
wait for the purposefully ignorant like a crocodile waits in the
bog. She is the mystery of life that can never be mastered; she
grows more menacing with every retreat.[142]

The Destructive Mother is the negative aspect of the unknown.
She is all things that destroy, entropy, and decay. She is the source of
all natural disasters, fatal diseases, and bloodthirsty predators. She is
the terrifying unknown and an agent of the Dragon of Chaos. In fact,
the Dragon of Chaos—or the Serpent of Chaos—can often be seen
lurking behind the Destructive Mother, which is why she typically
manifests reptilian or birdlike features.[143]

The terrible feminine has been represented by figures such as
the chimera, the sphinx, the griffin and the gorgon . . . Gor-
gon-like figures and their "sisters" appear commonly throughout
the world. As the Aztec *Coatlicue,* whose gruesome headdress
was composed of skulls, the Terrible Mother was goddess of
death and dismemberment, object of sacrificial homage. As
Goddess of the Snake, she was sacred in ancient Crete, and
worshiped by the Romans. Her modern equivalents remain
extant in Bali and India. *Kali,* Hindu goddess, is eight-armed,
like a spider, and sits within a web of fire. Each of her arms
bears a tool of creation or weapon of destruction. She wears
a tiara of skulls, has pointed, phallic breasts, and aggressive,
staring eyes. A snake, symbol of ancient, impersonal power,
transformation and rebirth, is coiled around her waist. She
simultaneously devours, and gives birth, to a full-grown man.
Medusa, Greek monster, with her coif of snakes, manifests a
visage so terrible that a single exposure turns strong men to
stone—paralyzes them, permanently, with fear. This gorgon
is a late "vestigial" remnant, so to speak, of an early goddess,
who simultaneously embodied nature's incredible productive
fecundity and callous disregard for life.[144]

Figure 8.4

Figure 8.5

Kali **(Fig. 8.4 and Fig. 8.5)**[145] is the Hindu representation of the Destructive Mother, the negative aspect of the unknown, and she is our ancestor's attempt to represent *everything that you should run away from screaming* into a single image.[146]

The Destructive Mother is the human-octopus hybrid, Ursula, in *The Little Mermaid*, who makes crooked deals with "poor unfortunate souls." She is Maleficent in *Sleeping Beauty*, the "Mistress of All Evil," who places a curse on Princess Aurora as a punishment for not being invited to her christening. She is the Red Queen in *Alice In Wonderland*, the destructive aspect of nature who constantly screams, "Off with their heads!" and tells Alice, "In my kingdom you have to run as fast as you can just to stay in the same place."[147] The Destructive Mother is the Wicked Witch of the West in *The Wizard Of Oz*, who cackles at Dorothy, "I'll get you, my pretty, and your little dog too!" She is the witch who fattens children with the intent of eating them in *Hansel and Gretel*, Cinderella's evil stepmother, and Creulla de Vil in *101 Dalmatians*. The Destructive Mother is the negative aspect of nature that surrounds the walls of culture and tries to sneak in every chance she gets. She stalks us and patiently waits for the right moment to strike, and there is no hiding from her fury.

The unknown is the source of all new things, as well as the place where all things eventually return. It is a place full of both hope and fear, wisdom and terror, creation and destruction. The unknown is the domain of chaos itself, and it is represented in mythology by the *Creative and Destructive Mothers*—two sides of the same coin, who together make up a totality.

The characters of mythology represent the fundamental elements of human existence. The Dragon of Chaos represents the precosmogonic chaos—the ultimate unknown, and field of potential from which everything arises. He hides gold and guards virgins, and if given the chance, will destroy us in an instant. Then there is unexplored territory, a smaller, more understandable form of chaos. This unknown is represented by the Great Mother; the Good Mother who nourishes, and the Terrible Mother who devours. It is the Great Mother who surrounds the walls of culture and waits for the right moment to show her face. Culture—explored territory—is represented in mythology as order and is portrayed by the Great Father, the Wise King who disciplines and fosters the growth of his children, and the Evil Tyrant who imprisons and suffocates them. And in the middle of it all lies the individual—the main character who experiences the world and determines how everything will unfold.

## Recap

- Explored and unexplored territory are represented in mythology as order and chaos.
- The totality of human experience is portrayed in mythology in the following way: the precosmogonic chaos gives rise to everything. The individual is protected by order and surrounded by chaos.
- Humans are social creatures, and therefore experience the world as if it were personified.
- Humans use social categories to understand this personified world.
- Our primary social categories are *father, mother, the individual, and predator.*
- The precosmogonic chaos is the field of potential that gives rise to everything. It is the ultimate unknown, and can either destroy us, or provide us with life transforming information. The precosmogonic chaos is represented in mythology as the Dragon of Chaos, the ultimate predator who guards something of value.
- Order is represented as the Great Father. The Protective Father is the beneficial aspect of order, and the Tyrannical Father is the destructive aspect.
- Chaos is represented as the Great Mother. The Creative Mother is the beneficial aspect of chaos, and the Destructive Mother is the destructive aspect.

CHAPTER NINE

# The Players of Mythology - Part Two

THE LAST FUNDAMENTAL ELEMENT OF human existence is you, the individual—the "child" of Mother Nature and Father Culture. The individual is the person who is always there for you no matter what; they are the anonymous donation and the encouraging word; the creators of disease-curing medicines, and of life-changing inventions; the individual is he or she who pursues truth above all things and seeks justice in the face of eminent threat; the person who runs into burning buildings in hopes of saving just one more person.

But the individual is not all sunshine and rainbows, for he also has a darker side. That is, the individual is not only the helping-hand and the shoulder to cry on, but he is also the liar, the cheat, the murderer, and the rapist; the one who wants the innocent to suffer and the world to burn. He is the mastermind behind the concentration camp and the gulag, as well as the creator of chemical warfare and the hydrogen bomb. The individual is he who seeks destruction on the world, and then revels in its devastation.

Like all elements of existence, the individual has both a positive and a negative aspect and is therefore represented in mythology by two distinct characters: *the hero and the adversary*.

# The Hero

First, we acted in the world. Then we watched ourselves act and told stories about how we were acting. As time progressed, we began to notice that some people did better in life than others; that some people consistently brought forth good things from the unknown. Naturally, we admired these people and told stories about what they were doing. And as we continued to tell stories about these successful people, we began to realize that they had certain things in common, a realization that eventually led to us taking the commonalities of these successful people—that is, extracting out the spirit of their behaviors and attitudes—and condensing them into one single character, the hero.

The hero is the beneficial aspect of the individual. He is a collection of attitudes and behaviors that *work*. He is the personality that brings forth good things from the unknown, and simultaneously guards against the tyranny of culture. He is the master of tradition and the spirit of progress. He is what pays attention and updates maps. He is the saving grace that rescues the world from destruction.

## I. What Makes a Hero?

Because it is impossible to know everything, we will inevitably fall into chaos at some point in our lives. But when this happens, there is still hope. When we fall into the unknown, there is still a chance we might actually learn something new; a chance that we can use the information we find in the unknown to update our maps and rise back up even stronger than before. To understand this is to understand that the information we find in the unknown is *redemptive* in nature, meaning it gives us a second chance; it allows us to grow instead of crumble, to rise instead of fall, to move forward instead of sinking farther into darkness.

The hero is the individual who strives to make things better; he who wants to bring about good things and therefore is willing to sacrifice everything to make that happen. And because it is redemptive knowledge that allows us to generate good things from the unknown, a perfect description of the hero is: *he who values and pursues redemptive knowledge above all things.*

By striving to make things better—that is, by pursuing redemptive knowledge above all things—the hero typically manifests certain qualities. For starters, when we learn from our mistakes we usually become wiser, and it is this wisdom that allows us to grow more competent and go on to generate good things.[148] This means that, in a sense, redemptive knowledge actually *is* wisdom.[149] And not only that, but the pursuit of wisdom could also be considered an act of wisdom itself.[150] Which means that by pursuing redemptive knowledge, the hero simultaneously possesses a level of wisdom that he otherwise would not have had.

By seeking redemptive knowledge, the hero not only displays wisdom, but he also embraces an attitude of humility. When we value and pursue redemptive knowledge above all things, we are essentially acknowledging that we don't know everything there is to know; we are recognizing that we might be wrong about what we think, and in doing so, giving ourselves a chance to learn something new.[151] The hero is the individual who values the truth over being right, which means he is willing to be wrong and thought of as a fool in order to obtain redemptive knowledge. This is why psychoanalyst Carl Jung believed the fool was a precursor to the hero. Whenever we begin to learn a new skill, we are usually completely lost and useless—that is, a fool. But when we give ourselves permission to be fools, we are simultaneously giving ourselves permission to learn new things. And if we remain fools for long enough, we will eventually learn to become masters. Therefore, by valuing and pursuing redemptive knowledge above all things we acknowledge our limitations and ultimately put ourselves in a position to learn and succeed.

Such "ideas" are well illustrated in the Brothers Grimm fairy tale *The Water of Life*:

> *There once was a king who was so ill that it was thought impossible his life could be saved. He had three sons, and they were all in great distress on his account, and they went into the castle gardens and wept at the thought that he must die. An old man came up to them and asked the cause of their grief. They told him that their father was dying, and nothing could save him.*

*The old man said, "There is only one remedy which
I know. It is the Water of Life. If he drinks of it he will
recover, but it is very difficult to find."*

The two eldest sons determine to seek out the Water of Life,
one after the other, after gaining their father's reluctant permission. They both encounter a dwarf, at the beginning of their
journeys, and speak rudely to him. The dwarf places a curse
on them, and they each end up stuck fast in a mountain gorge.

The "youngest son" then sets out. He is humble and has the
"right attitude" toward what he does not understand. When he
encounters the dwarf, therefore... he receives some valuable
information:

*"As you have spoken pleasantly to me, and not been haughty
like your false brothers, I will help you and tell you how
to find the Water of Life. It flows from a fountain in the
courtyard of an enchanted castle. But you will never get
in unless I give you an iron rod and two loaves of bread.
With the rod strike three times on the iron gate of the castle
and it will spring open. Inside you will find two lions with
wide-open jaws, but if you throw a loaf to each they will
be quiet. Then you must make haste to fetch the Water of
Life before it strikes twelve, or the gates of the castle will
close, and you will be shut in."*

The story is making a point: when you don't know where you
are going, it is counterproductive to assume that you know how
to get there. This point is a specific example of a more general
moral: Arrogant ("prideful") individuals presume they know
who and what is important. This makes them too haughty
to pay attention when they are in trouble—too haughty, in
particular, to attend to those things or people whom they
habitually hold in contempt.[152]

Next, it turns out that redemptive information—the information
that we need the most—is usually found where we least want to

look.[153] If that wasn't the case, nothing would have deterred us from finding it in the first place. This is why when King Arthur's knights go looking for the Holy Grail—an artifact of ultimate value—each knight begins their quest by entering the forest at a point which looks darkest to *him*.[154] Ultimately, this means that valuing and pursuing redemptive knowledge above all things is also an act of courage. To acknowledge that we don't know everything is a terrifying endeavor because it means we might eventually have to change who we are and what we believe; it means we might have to eventually sacrifice a part of ourselves that we would rather keep. This means that when the hero pursues redemptive knowledge, he does not identify with anything concrete—like his job, political beliefs, or social status—but rather, *he identifies with the process of transformation itself*. Before we can become someone new, we first have to let go of who we are; which is to say, in order for us to grow, old parts of ourselves first have to die.[155] This means that when the hero identifies with the process of transformation, he is essentially identifying with a process of death and rebirth.

Also, as a consequence of constantly searching for redemptive information, we find that the hero typically values the *spirit* of the rules—which is the underlying essence and purpose of the rules—over the actual rules themselves. This is why the hero is typically portrayed in stories as a rule breaker.[156] By aiming at making things better, the hero is willing to break the rules in service of some higher good; he places truth over dogma[157] and serves the spirit that the rules were meant to honor in the first place. The hero recognizes that no rule is meant to be followed blindly, and when he finds that the rules are not serving their purpose, he breaks them in an attempt to update them. And it is this willingness of the hero to break the rules that makes him a revolutionary figure of sorts—a true individual who is willing to step outside of the group and follow his conscience.[158]

> Application of the letter of the law when the spirit of the law is necessary makes mockery of culture. Following in the footsteps of others seems safe, and requires no thought—but it is useless to follow a well-trodden trail when the terrain itself

has changed. The individual who fails to modify his habits and presumptions as a consequence of change is deluding himself—is denying the world—is trying to replace reality itself with his own feeble wish. By pretending things are other than they are, he undermines his own stability, destabilizes his future, and transforms the past from shelter to prison. . . .[159]

The actions and attitudes of J.K. Rowling's heroes and heroines once again provide popular examples of precisely this process. Harry Potter, Ron Weasley, and Hermione Granger are typified in large part by the willingness and ability to follow rules (indicating their expertise as apprentices) and, simultaneously, to break them. . . .

There is a strong implication throughout the series that what is good cannot be simply encapsulated by mindless or rigid rule following, no matter how disciplined that following, or how vital the rules so followed. What this all means is that the Harry Potter series does not point to drone-like subservience to social order as the highest of moral virtues. What supersedes that obedience is not so obvious that it can be easily articulated, but it is something like "Follow rules except when doing so undermines the purpose of those selfsame rules—in which case take the risk of acting in a manner contrary to what has been agreed upon as moral."[160]

By striving to make things better, the hero embraces an attitude of wisdom, humility, and courage; he chooses to identify with the process of transformation and ends up serving the spirit of truth above all things. And as a result, he gives himself the best chance to successfully overcome the darkness of chaos and save the world.

## II. The Hero's Journey

As we move through life we will inevitably fall into chaos, but it is within this domain of chaos that we will find life-changing information; information that will allow us to rebuild our maps and rise back up even stronger than before. Herein lies the story of mankind—a story of death and rebirth that is represented in mythology as *the hero's journey.*

Although variations of the hero myth are found all over the world, they all seem to maintain a similar structure: a harmonious community or way of life is unexpectedly threatened by the emergence of some unknown dangerous force. An individual of humble and/or princely origins decides to voluntarily confront this threat, and over the course of his journey, faces many trials and hardships. Eventually, this individual overcomes the threat, is magically restored or improved as a result, and receives a reward that he ends up taking back to his community, ultimately reestablishing harmonious order.[161]

The most primordial threat is the sudden (re)appearance or discovery of one of the manifestations of the Terrible Mother: a flood, an earthquake, a war, a monster (some type of dragon), a fish, a whale—anything unpredictable or unexpected that destroys, devours, traps, engulfs, dismembers, tortures, terrifies, weakens, mystifies, entrances, smothers or poisons (this is a partial list). The hero, product of divine parentage and miraculous birth, survivor of a dangerous childhood, faces the Terrible Mother in single combat and is devoured. He is swallowed by a great fish, or snake, or whale, and spends time underground, in the the dark, in the winter, in the kingdom of the dead, or in hell; faces a dragon, a gorgon, a witch or temptress; is inundated by water, by fire, by storm, by dangerous animals; is tormented, buried alive, mesmerized, dismembered, disemboweled and deluded. He defeats the monster, freeing those who had previously been defeated, and gains or regains a lost or previously undiscovered object of value, a (virginal) woman or a treasure. Much older, much wiser, he returns home, transformed in character, bearing what he has gained, and reunites himself triumphantly with his community, which is much enriched—or even utterly transformed—by his fortune.[162]

Perhaps the hero myth that our culture is most familiar with is the myth of *Saint George and the Dragon* **(see Fig. 9.1)**.[163] In this myth, St. George voluntarily confronts and slays a dragon who has been terrorizing a nearby village. He then rescues the princess this dragon has imprisoned—a virginal figure representing the creative and fertile aspect of the unknown—and brings her back to the village. Other variations of this story have the hero slaying the dragon and returning with some sort of treasure, a reference to the valuable redemptive knowledge that can be found in the unknown if it is approached correctly.

**Figure 9.1:** The battle of the hero is a frequent motif in mythologically inspired sculpture, drawing and painting. A representative example is presented in [the figure above]. All of the elements of the "meta-myth" are portrayed in this drawing: the threatened community, represented by the walled city or castle; the winged dragon, who has emerged from the underworld (and whose lair is surrounded by the bones of the dead); the hero, armed with the sword, who "cuts" the leviathan into pieces, and makes the world [out of those pieces]; and the virgin, freed from the dragon's clutches, who represents the benevolent, creative and fruitful aspect of the unknown. (The city is commonly portrayed on a mountain, in such representations—the serpent in a valley, or across a river.)[164]

---

The legend of *St. George and the Dragon* illustrates one of the most important rules in psychotherapy: if we want to improve the quality of our lives, we have to voluntarily confront the things we are afraid of.[165] And although this legend is one of the oldest stories of mankind, it is by no means outdated. In fact, variations of this story can be found everywhere. For instance, take J. R. R. Tolkien's *The Hobbit*. In *The Hobbit*, a great dragon named Smaug forces a community of dwarves out of their kingdom and steals their stockpile of gold. As the story progresses, a hobbit—which is basically a smaller version of a human—by the name of Bilbo Baggins is recruited to help the dwarves take back their kingdom from this fire-breathing dragon. Over the course of his journey, Bilbo overcomes many trials and tribulations; he eventually helps the dwarves defeat Smaug, reestablishing the dwarf kingdom and, as a payment for his help, is rewarded a portion of the dwarves gold, at which point he returns home with his treasure in hand.

The legend of Saint George and the Dragon can also be found in the second edition of J. K. Rowling's Harry Potter series, *Harry Potter & the Chamber of Secrets*. Rowling's story begins with Harry Potter returning to Hogwarts—a school that teaches magic to young witches and wizards—after his summer vacation. Hogwarts represents order and the known; it is the walls of culture that create a safe and predictable environment so that those within its walls can grow and flourish. Now, as the story unfolds, we learn that beneath the school is a secret chamber containing a basilisk—a giant snake with a gaze so lethal that it instantly kills those who make eye contact with it—and a student by the name of Ginevra Weasley has been captured by the basilisk and taken down to its lair.

Determined to save Ginevra, Harry Potter voluntarily descends beneath the school—that is, he descends into the underworld—on a mission to confront the basilisk. And after much searching, he eventually finds the Chamber of Secrets, battles the basilisk, and kills it, only to find that he has been fatally bitten by one of its poisonous fangs in the process. And as a doomed Harry Potter lies beneath the school awaiting his fate, a phoenix—a bird that the ancient Egyptians used to symbolize the process of death and rebirth[166]—flies into the Chamber of Secrets and heals Harry by crying tears into his wounds. This allows Harry to resurface from the underworld with Ginevra—Ginevra being another name for *Virginia*, which is a variant of *Virgin*—by his side.[167]

"There's nothing about it that's rational. Nothing! Magic castle? That's not rational. Giant snake underneath it? . . . Going down there to face it and being rejuvenated by a Phoenix? It's like 'Yeah, that's okay! We'll watch that! We'll swallow it! We'll be completely engaged in it!' And the reason for that is because it's a myth. It's a meta-story about how to act; about how to conduct yourself in the world and face the things that you're afraid of.[168]

"The mythological substructure upon which the Harry Potter volumes are based are drawing from these same underlying pool of ideas and symbols. They're universally accessible. You can tell that because if they weren't, that book wouldn't have sold—how many millions of copies did it sell? And the movies? It's unbelievable. Overwhelmingly powerful. *She got kids to read six-hundred-page books!* Multiple volumes! Lined up for them! You've got to ask yourself why. 'Silly stories about magical orphans.' It's like, well . . . maybe not."[169]

Fundamentally, *Harry Potter & the Chamber of Secrets* is a story about death and rebirth. It is a story that says, "What saves you from an encounter with the Dragon of Chaos is your willingness to let yourself die and come back to life";[170] or said another way, "The part of you that is willing to die and resurrect, is what will rescue the virgin [the beneficial aspect of the unknown] from the snake."[171]

Ultimately, the hero is a compilation of attitudes and behaviors that guard against the tyranny of culture, while simultaneously producing good things from the unknown. The hero is he who aims at making things better by committing himself to the spirit of truth; the individual who voluntarily confronts the unknown, gains something of value, and brings it back to the community; he who identifies with the process of transformation, and in doing so, embraces death so that he may live.

The hero is Simba from *The Lion King*, the rightful heir of Pride Rock who must first be transformed within the heart of a dark forest before he can save his kingdom from tyranny. He is Pinocchio, the puppet who must die rescuing his father from a whale before he can become a real boy. He is J. K. Rowling's Harry Potter, Bilbo Baggins from *The Hobbit*, and Prince Phillip in *Sleeping Beauty*, the prince who must defeat a fire-breathing dragon in order to rescue princess Aurora.

According to mythology, how the hero approaches the unknown influences what aspect of it will manifest. If we approach the unknown voluntarily—that is, *as if it is beneficial*—then mythology claims it is more likely we will experience it in a positive way.[172] This is the fundamental and truly revolutionary hypothesis of mankind: *that life can be improved (and should be improved) by the voluntary change of an individual's attitude and actions.*[173] This is not to say that an attitude change will stop bad things from ever happening to us, but rather it is to say that how we choose to respond to these bad things will determine if life gets better or worse.

The hero is mankind's attempt to represent how we should live if we want to make things better; he is a compilation of attitudes and actions that have been proven to work over time. The hero is a hypothesis; he is mankind's bet on reality. And this hypothesis claims that by attempting to make things better—by valuing and pursuing redemptive knowledge above all things—we give ourselves the best chance to *actually* make things better. If we voluntarily and courageously confront the unknown, then we may actually defeat the Dragon of Chaos in our lives and obtain something of value in the process.[174]

## The Adversary

Like the hero, the adversary is also a collection of attitudes and behaviors that have been condensed into a single character and passed down through the art of storytelling. The character of the adversary portrays the destructive aspect of the individual; the part of us that feels cheated by life and seeks retaliation; the part that wants other people to suffer because we have suffered. It is who we see when we observe the many atrocities committed by mankind over the course of history; it is who plans the rape and genocide of entire populations, and the one who invents new methods of torture, humiliation, and execution. The adversary is he who desires to make things worse instead of better; he who does *not* value and pursue redemptive knowledge above all things. In fact, the adversary denies the existence of redemptive knowledge altogether and, therefore, rejects the beneficial aspect of the unknown entirely—the very thing that could save him from his misery.

Now the adversary, like the hero, has also been known to manifest certain qualities of his own. For starters, by denying redemptive information, the adversary claims omniscience and implicitly states, "I already know everything there is to know." But knowing everything means that there is no unknown, and consequently no treasure to be found. This ultimately leads to the adversary rejecting the process of transformation altogether, and thus any chance he has of becoming the hero.[175] As a result, whenever the adversary comes into contact with information that invalidates his map of the world, he turns away; he hides his eyes and refuses to acknowledge that his current understanding of the world may be flawed, and in doing so, he *embraces the lie.*

As a consequence of believing he has nothing left to learn, the adversary adopts an attitude of arrogance and pride—qualities that are often rooted in an individual's belief in their own intelligence, which may account for why so many villains are depicted as evil geniuses.

If we are smart enough, we can rationalize anything we want. But unchecked rationality usually ends up deceiving the individual into believing that his or her ideas about the world are flawless. Thus, rationality suffers from the greatest of temptations: the tendency to fall in love with its own creations. A high rational intelligence can cause the individual to create a theory about the world, and then to believe that theory is one hundred percent correct. And if a theory is one hundred percent correct, any challenge to that theory can be justifiably eliminated. This is how the adversary naturally falls into totalitarian thinking and behaviors.[176]

Not only is the denial of redemptive information an act of pride, but it is also the way of the coward. It is fear, rather than confidence, that causes the adversary to cling to his current beliefs and insist he possesses absolute knowledge. It is fear of his own shortcomings, fear of what redemptive information might mean for change, that causes him to reject the truth. But by rejecting redemptive information and claiming omniscience, the adversary denies the opportunity to become a true individual. By looking down on those who are willing to be the fool, he refuses the humility necessary for becoming the hero and, therefore, rejects any chance he has of making things better.

The adversary lies to himself about his own experiences and does whatever it takes to keep his lies alive. But lying only makes things worse. Because he refuses to learn anything new, the adversary does not grow stronger. In fact, every time the adversary denies redemptive information he gets weaker and more dependent on his lies to hide his inadequacies and in doing so, he ensures that his interactions with the unknown will *never* produce good things. And once an individual severs any chance he has of experiencing good things, all that will remain is pain and suffering. As result of feeling cheated by life, the individual will grow angry and resentful, which will then cause things to go from bad to worse, turning tragedy into hell.[177]

Hell is the land of misery, and misery loves company. While in hell, the adversary bathes in his anger and resentment, causing him to hate those whom life has seemed to favor. In his misery he thinks, "*Life has been so unfair and cruel to me that it would be better if it had never existed at all.*" It is in this moment that the adversary's cowardice, pride, and resentment cause him to justify seeking revenge on life itself; it is in this moment that the adversary commits himself to the spirit of evil.

> Hell comes when lies have destroyed the relationship between individual or state and reality itself. Things fall apart. Life degenerates. Everything becomes frustration and disappointment. Hope consistently betrays. . . . Then the drama enters its final act.
>
> Tortured by constant failure, the individual becomes bitter. Disappointment and failure amalgamate, and produce a fantasy: *the world is bent on my personal suffering, my particular undoing, my destruction.* I need, I deserve, I must have—my revenge.[178]

## I. Evil

Modern people often roll their eyes when they hear the word *evil* because they feel it is outdated and has religious implications. But this is a serious mistake. Evil is by no means outdated. And perhaps the word has religious connotations, but that is mainly because religious language is the only type of language capable of describing something so dark and horrific.

So what exactly is evil? For starters, evil is not tragedy. Tragedy is something that we will inevitably experience due to the fact we are vulnerable[179] (we not only can get sick and die, but we can also watch our loved ones do the same). Natural disasters, diseases, and untimely accidents are not evil, they are merely the price we pay for being alive—evil is something else entirely.

There is a type of suffering that extends far beyond mere tragedy and is therefore in need of a category of its own. And the things that belong to this category—the category of evil—are all defined by one thing, and one thing only: *consciousness*. Evil is a choice; it is something that can only come into the world through a conscious decision, which makes evil something completely unique to human beings.

Tragedy alone is not evil, it is just the way things are. Evil is the conscious intention to cause someone else unnecessary suffering purely for the sake of that suffering; it is the attitude that revels in using one's imagination to wreak havoc on the world.

"It's more appropriate to consider evil as a form of demonically warped aesthetic. . . . The motto on the gates of Auschwitz in the Second World War was *Work Will Make You Free*—that's another manifestation of the aesthetic of evil. It's a terrible, terrible, ironic joke. And it's instructive to meditate on what sort of imagination would have the arrogance to tell such a terrible joke.[180]

"Once they were in Auschwitz, the guards use to play tricks on the prisoners. One trick would be to get some poor son of a bitch who had just been torn away from his country, had his family destroyed, who knew where he was going, who was half dead for six different reasons, who was among strangers . . . and they'd give him wet sacks of salt—which would weigh about a hundred pounds—and they'd have him carry them from one side of the compound to the other . . . and then carry them back![181] And when you think of a camp you think of something like a football field. . . . No way, man. *These were cities*; there were tens of thousands of people in these places. So from one side of the compound to the other—that was a good hike. And if that wasn't enough, they'd get them to carry it back and put it in the same place. Now that's poetic in its malevolence. What you're doing is you're harnessing the human compulsion to engage in a useful activity, and demonstrating how absolutely futile it is despite its difficulty.[182]

"This is something you're going to have to understand if you really want to understand evil: evil is an aesthetic; *it's an art form.*[183] It's a celebration of horror. It's a conscious attempt to violate the conditions that make life itself tolerable. It's aimed at dehumanization and destruction of the ideal. And at an even deeper level, it's revenge against the conditions of existence itself."[184]

In the early twentieth century, there was a serial killer and rapist by the name of Carl Panzram. To put it mildly, Panzram had a very hard and unfair childhood. When he was a young boy he was sent off to a reform school where we was brutalized and raped by the people who were suppose to be taking care of him. And as a result, Panzram decided that there was nothing valuable about humanity and that he would cause as much devastation and destruction as he possibly could for the rest of his life.

Carl Panzram killed dozens of people and raped over one thousand men. He committed thousands of burglaries, robberies, and arsons, and kept track of the dollar amount of the buildings he burned down. The man was hell-bent on destruction and, luckily, was eventually caught, tried, and sentenced to death. As he awaited his execution date, a human rights activist group offered to intervene on his behalf, but he refused their help by replying, "The only thanks you and your kind will ever get from me for your efforts on my behalf is that I wish you all had one neck and that I had my hands on it." Finally, the day came for Panzram to be hanged. And his last words to the hangman? "Hurry up, you Hoosier bastard, I could kill ten men while you're fooling around."[185]

Evil is a choice that the adversary feels justified in making. He feels cheated by life and therefore embraces an attitude of vengeance. The adversary is Scar in the *Lion King*, brother of King Mufasa. Scar believes that life has done him an injustice; he believes he deserves to be king, and that although he is unmatched in intelligence, his lack of good genetics—the type of genetics that has been arbitrarily gifted to his brother—has cost him the crown. As a result of his resentment, Scar murders his brother, seizes the crown for himself, and lays waste to the Pride Lands (it is worth noting that the Tyrannical Father and the adversary can sometimes be played by the same character, as the negative aspect of the individual is usually what gives rise to the tyrannical aspect of culture).

The adversary also makes an appearance as the coachman in *Pinocchio*, a man who turns young boys into donkeys and sells them into slavery for his own gain. He is Lex Luther from *Superman*, an evil genius who believes his intelligence gives him the right to rule the world. He is the Joker in *Batman*, Magneto in *X-Men*, and Lord Voldemort in *Harry Potter*. He is also Anakin Skywalker—soon to be Darth Vader—in *Star Wars*, the Jedi Knight who allows his anger, hatred, and resentment to fuel his justifications for joining the dark side and killing Jedi children.

The adversary is he who does not value and pursue redemptive knowledge above all things. He is the individual who wants to make things worse, instead of better. He rejects the truth by denying his own experience, by denying the unknown, and ultimately severs his ties with all beneficial things. The adversary arrogantly believes he can manipulate the world and get away with it. He is the attitude and personality that scoffs at the fool; that rejects the process of transformation and, therefore, any chance he has of becoming the hero. Through his pride and resentment, the adversary turns tragedy into hell and then seeks to force this hell on the rest of the world.

**"When we look at people like Stalin and Hitler we think they were after world domination. . . . I don't have any idea why we would ever assume those guys were after victory. You should never make the assumption that everyone is out to win. Some people are out to lose, and the more people they can take with them, the better.**

**"When Hitler died he committed suicide in a bunker way down below Berlin when Berlin was on fire and Europe was burning. As far as I can tell, that's exactly what Hitler was after right from the beginning. . . . Why we would assume that he wanted to win just because that's what he said is**

something I've never been able to understand. The kids who shot up Columbine didn't want to win. They wanted to kill as many people as possible to make a point. And then they wanted to kill themselves *just in case you didn't exactly get the point.* The point was, 'The more destruction the better. And if I have to go along with it, no problem. That just makes me a little bit more serious than I would have otherwise been.' And so those sorts of motivations are not pleasant to understand but we have enough documentation of events like that, especially the mass killings—those guys have written down exactly why they do it."[186]

## Batman—*The Dark Knight Rises*

### BRUCE WAYNE

Criminals aren't complicated, Alfred. We just need to figure out what he's after.

### ALFRED

With respect, Master Wayne, perhaps this is a man that you don't fully understand, either. A long time ago, I was in Burma. My friends and I were working for the local government. We were trying to buy the loyalty of tribal leaders by bribing them with precious stones. But their caravans were being raided in a forest north of Rangoon by a bandit. So we went looking for the stones. But in six months, we never met anyone who had traded with him. One day I saw a child playing with a ruby the size of a tangerine . . . The bandit had been throwing the stones away.

### BRUCE WAYNE

So why steal them?

**ALFRED**

Well, because he thought it was good sport. Because some men aren't looking for anything logical, like money. They can't be bought, bullied, reasoned, or negotiated with. Some men just want to watch the world burn.

When bad things happen we find ourselves at a fork in the road. Do we curse life and seek revenge, or do we aim at something higher? Do we attempt to make things worse, or do we attempt to make them better? Ultimately, this is the choice that defines humanity; within each of us exists both a hero and an adversary, and it is up to us to choose which character we are going to play.

## Recap

- The individual has both a positive and negative aspect and, therefore, is represented in mythology by two characters: the hero and the adversary.
- The hero represents the beneficial aspect of the individual—the attitudes and actions that work.
- The hero is he or she who values and pursues redemptive knowledge above all things, and in doing so, manifests traits that allow the beneficial aspect of the unknown to be revealed; traits such as wisdom, humility, and courage.
- By valuing and pursuing redemptive knowledge above all things, the hero identifies with the process of transformation—that is, the process of death and rebirth.
- By valuing and pursuing redemptive knowledge above all things, the hero places the spirit of truth over dogma and, as a result, is often portrayed as a rule breaker and revolutionary figure.
- The hero's journey depicts the fundamental story of mankind: the hero confronts the unknown (or tyranny of culture), gains something of value, and (re)creates the world from this encounter (i.e., brings what was gained back to the community and reestablishes order).
- The hero's journey is mankind's hypothesis on how to live successfully. It claims that how we approach the unknown will actually

determine how it manifests. That is, if we desire to make things better—if we value and pursue redemptive knowledge above all things—then we will actually have a better chance of experiencing good things.

- The adversary is the destructive aspect of the individual—he or she who does not value and pursue redemptive knowledge of all things and, therefore, stops the beneficial aspect of the unknown from manifesting.
- By denying redemptive information, the adversary commits to the lie and embraces an attitude of pride, arrogance, and cowardice.
- Evil is an art form; it is the intention of causing someone else unnecessary suffering for the sake of that suffering.
- Feeling cheated by life, the adversary justifies committing acts of evil and seeks revenge on the world.
- The hero wants to make things better, while the adversary wants to make things worse.

CHAPTER TEN

# The Enuma Elish

Mankind has been telling stories to one another for thousands of years. We began by watching ourselves act and telling stories about how we were acting; we watched the people around us and told stories about those who courageously confronted the unknown and succeeded, as well as about those who looked tyranny in the face and said, "No." We told stories about good versus evil—about the two paths we all face, and where exactly each path leads. And as time progressed, the stories that people found most helpful were passed down through generations and kept alive, while everything else was cast aside and forgotten.

A highly functioning civilization is always propped up by a set of values, values which can usually be found within the stories of that civilization. In the West, many of the values we hold to be self-evident were not always so. In fact, many of the ideas that we believe are common sense today have gone through an incredibly lengthy period of development. Therefore, if we really want to understand the values of our own culture, we should try and understand where these ideas originated and how they developed over time.

We will begin by looking at an ancient Mesopotamian creation myth, the *Enuma elish*. The Enuma elish is one of the oldest, if not *the* oldest, written stories that we know of, and since it is a Middle Eastern story, and all of the Abrahamic religions emerged out of the Middle East, it is also a story that sits at the very foundation of our own culture.[187]

## The Enuma Elish

Like all ancient civilizations, the Mesopotamians did not view the world through a scientific lens and therefore were not interested in scientific explanations for how the world was created. According to the Mesopotamian creation myth, the *Enuma elish*, in the beginning there was a swirling chaos of two primordial waters. And these two waters—one fresh water and one salt water—were deities that were intermingled together in a sexual and creative embrace. The fresh water deity was named Apsu—the Great Father who served as the protective and tyrannical aspects of order—and the saltwater deity was a dragon named Tiamat—the Great Mother who served as the beneficial and destructive aspects of chaos. Together, masculine Apsu and feminine Tiamat were the source of all things—that is, the precosmogonic chaos—and therefore, their embrace can be conceptualized as a uroboros **(see Fig. 10.1, Fig. 10.2, and Fig. 10.3).**[188]

As the story goes, the divine parents, Apsu and Tiamat, give birth to gods. But unfortunately for Apsu and Tiamat, these gods turn out to be incredibly annoying—they are wild, careless, and impulsive deities; they are constantly getting into mischief and make so much noise that Apsu and Tiamat have trouble sleeping at night. This racket goes on for some time until a frustrated Apsu decides he is going to kill his children so that he and Tiamat can finally get some much needed rest. But upon hearing this, the god Ea strikes first and kills Apsu, and then, weirdly enough, builds a dwelling place on top of Apsu's corpse:

> *He bound Apsû and killed him;*
> *Mummu he confined and handled roughly.*
> *He set his dwelling upon Apsû,*
> *And laid hold on Mummu, keeping the nose-rope in his hand.*
> *After Ea had bound and slain his enemies,*
> *Had achieved victory over his foes,*
> *He rested quietly in his chamber,*
> *He called it Apsû, whose shrines he appointed.*
> *Then he founded his living-quarters within it.*[189]

Figure 10.1

Figure 10.2                    Figure 10.3

But as the gods soon learn, once the walls of culture are torn down, there is nothing left to protect them from the flood of chaos. When the female dragon-deity, Tiamat, learns of her husband's murder, she loses her mind in a fit of rage, and makes it her mission to extermi-nate her children once and for all. Preparing for war, Tiamat builds herself an army full of terrifying monsters and places her new lover, Kingu (Qingu), at the head of her army and gives him the Tablet of Destinies—something that gives him authority to rule over the universe and determine destinies.

*Lusting for battle, raging, storming,*
*They set up a host to bring about conflict.*
*Mother Hubur [Tiamat], who forms everything,*
*Supplied irresistible weapons, and gave birth to giant serpents.*
*They had sharp teeth, they were merciless . . . .*
*With poison instead of blood she filled their bodies.*
*She clothed the fearful monsters with dread,*
*She loaded them with an aura and made them godlike.*
*(She said,) "Let their onlooker feebly perish,*
*May they constantly leap forward and never retire."*
*She created the Hydra, the Dragon, the Hairy Hero*
*The Great Demon, the Savage Dog, and the Scorpion-man,*
*Fierce demons, the Fish-man, and the Bull-man,*
*Carriers of merciless weapons, fearless in the face of battle.*
*Her commands were tremendous, not to be resisted.*
*Altogether she made eleven of that kind.*
*Among the gods, her sons, whom she constituted her host,*
*She exalted Qingu [Kingu], and magnified him among them.*
*The leadership of the army, the direction of the host,*
*The bearing of weapons, campaigning, the mobilization of conflict,*
*The chief executive power of battle, supreme command,*
*She entrusted to him and set him on a throne,*
*"I have cast the spell for you and exalted you in the host of the gods,*
*I have delivered to you the rule of all the gods.*
*You are indeed exalted, my spouse, you are renowned,*
*Let your commands prevail over all the Anunnaki."*
*She gave him the Tablet of Destinies and fastened it to his breast,*

*(Saying) "Your order may not be changed; let the utterance of your*
*mouth be firm."*[190]

Needless to say, when the gods see what's happening, they start to
freak out—they realize that if they don't stop Tiamat they are going
to be in serious trouble. Hoping they have someone in their ranks up
for the challenge, the gods send their best and brightest out to face
Tiamat and her army of monsters, only to find that they each come
crawling back, one by one, defeated and horror-stricken.

As the gods begin running out of options, and all hope seems to
be lost, someone says something like, "Hey, what about that new guy,
Marduk?" Now, Marduk is different from the other gods. For starters,
he's a new god, which means he is not the child of Apsu and Tiamat,
but rather, he is the progeny of the gods themselves. But what truly
makes Marduk unique is that he has four eyes and four ears—which
means he can see and hear everything—and he can also speak magic
words (it is said that flames shoot forth from his mouth and he can
speak both light and darkness into being). This means that Marduk
is not only something that can *really* pay attention, but he is also
something that can produce remarkable things with his speech.

*Four were his eyes, four his ears,*
*Flame shot forth as he moved his lips.*
*His four ears grew large,*
*And his eyes likewise took in everything.*[191]

So the gods ask Marduk if he would be willing to fight Tiamat,
an offer he only accepts under one condition: that the gods agree to
make him their ruler. Running out of options, the gods agree to grant
Marduk's request and form a council to officially announce him as top
god, ultimately representing a shift in Mesopotamia thinking from
polytheism towards monotheism.

Mesopotamia was a civilization that often incorporated other
tribes into their culture, tribes that usually had their own gods and
customs. Therefore, for the Mesopotamians, the question was, "If
we are all going to live together and get along, whose god is going
to be the most important; whose god are we going to follow?" And

as these tribes continued to fight it out and merge with one another, the gods and stories of these tribes merged together as well. And as a result, the Enuma elish emerged—a story that took the best and most important characteristics of each tribe's god and compiled them into one main god, Marduk.

> "Imagine a landscape that consists of tribes. And then on top of them, imagine a landscape of the imagination. Each member of a tribal group lives in their imagined world which is full of deities and natural forces of various kinds that they're following. But then imagine as these tribes battle it out and organize themselves, the figures in their imaginations do exactly the same thing. So as people are battling, the gods in heaven are battling—which is also very common in mythology. As human beings beat themselves into functional groups, their world conceptions do the same thing. So over time you move from polytheism, roughly speaking, to monotheism—these tribes communicate with one another in language, as well as through combat, and sort out exactly what should be held as sovereign, powerful, and dominant. . . .
>
> "This is reflected in the Mesopotamian creation myth. The gods assemble themselves and think, 'Someone here has the characteristics that should be the central element of the top deity.' So the Mesopotamians chose wisely: *vision and language*—those are the most potent weapons you have against chaos because if you pay attention, then you can see chaos when it first emerges, and if you are a master of language, then you can encapsulate it (articulate it very rapidly) and communicate it to other people. You cannot overestimate how radical of an idea that is! It's a staggeringly radical idea that those set of attributes should be at the top."[192]

And once he has been crowned top god, Marduk marches out to confront Tiamat and challenges her to a fight. As they wage war with one another, Marduk miraculously finds a way to trap Tiamat in a net—ultimately, it is Marduk's ability to see and speak that allows him to place borders around chaos and make her more manageable. By trapping Tiamat in a net, Marduk is attempting to define and pin down the chaos in front of him,[193] for a problem that is not acknowledged and properly articulated can never be solved. And once Tiamat has been subdued in a net, Marduk then blows wind into her belly, weighing her down, and fatally shoots her with an arrow.

*Be-l spread out his net and enmeshed her;*
*He let loose the Evil Wind, the rear guard, in her face.*
*Tia-mat opened her mouth to swallow it,*
*She let the Evil Wind in so that she could not close her lips.*
*The fierce winds weighed down her belly,*
*Her inwards were distended and she opened her mouth wide.*
*He let fly an arrow and pierced her belly,*
*He tore open her entrails and slit her inwards,*
*He bound her and extinguished her life,*
*He threw down her corpse and stood on it.[194]*

After Tiamat is defeated, a victorious Marduk then creates order out of chaos by cutting her body into pieces and using those pieces to make the world. Next, Marduk officially solidifies his place in the universe as top god by defeating Tiamat's army of monsters and taking the Tablet of Destinies from Kingu—which means that Marduk is now the set of attributes that has the authority to rule over the universe and determine destinies. And lastly, Marduk decides to make humans out of the blood of Kingu—a reference to the fact that humans are the only creatures in the world who have the capacity for evil[195]—and then declares the purpose of mankind is *to maintain the balance between chaos and order*.[196]

The Enuma elish is an attempt to figure something out. The Mesopotamians wanted to know which qualities were the most important for making things better, which qualities would turn chaos into order, and if embodied, would determine destinies. And after thousands of years of trial and error, the answer to their question emerged in a story.[197] The Mesopotamian creation myth hypothesizes that it is the *attention and speech* of an individual, as well as the courage to voluntarily confront the unknown, that allows them to succeed when they encounter the chaos in their lives. The Mesopotamians believed that the individual who paid attention and spoke the truth was someone who could take on an entire army of chaos and prevail; that once a problem was identified, the truth could cut that problem into manageable pieces, and those pieces could be used to (re)build the world.

Mesopotamia's decision to value attention and speech above all things was the very beginning of the idea of sovereignty, the beginning of the idea that there was something that should be regarded as having ultimate value and supreme authority. And as it turns out, the Mesopotamians believed that the individual who embodied these qualities—that is, *the individual who embodied Marduk*—was also considered sovereign by association. Now what's interesting is at that point in Mesopotamian history, the only person who identified as Marduk, and was therefore considered sovereign, was the emperor himself, because it was the emperor who consistently transformed chaos into order for the rest of Mesopotamia.

Every year during their New Year's celebration, as a way of honoring this principle of sovereignty, the Mesopotamians would take the emperor out of the city, remove his emperor clothes, and have him recall all the ways he had been a bad "Marduk" that year—that is, all the ways he had not properly transformed chaos into order.[198] This Mesopotamian ritual was merely a symptom of something much more profound; this ritual was the beginning of the idea that no matter who you were—whether you were a king, an emperor, or a prophet—there was something that existed above you that you had to answer to, an ideal above you that was worth honoring and striving for.

Marduk is the hero of Mesopotamian mythology and is referred to by fifty different names by the Mesopotamians[199]—one of which translates to *he who makes the ingenious things out of the conflict with Tiamat*.[200] And this is exactly what the hero does; the hero is he or she who courageously confronts the unknown and makes ingenious things out of chaos. And according to the Mesopotamians, the best way to do this is through paying attention and speaking the truth. This is what the Mesopotamians figured out—that our ability to pay attention and speak the truth is what will allow us to overcome the chaos in our lives. Now of course they didn't understand this idea in a conscious way, but rather, they understood it dramatically through rituals, images, and stories.

The Enuma elish is the Mesopotamian hypothesis about what set of attributes should be regarded as sovereign. And this hypothesis—something which took our ancestors thousands of years to figure out—is an idea that is still around today and underlies many of the stories found within our own culture. *Listen. Pay attention. Confront chaos and speak the truth.* This is the way forward. This is how we defeat the Dragon of Chaos and create a better world.

## Recap

- The Mesopotamian creation myth, the Enuma elish, is one of the oldest written stories that we know of and sits at the foundation of our culture.
- In the Enuma elish there is The Great Mother, as well as the Dragon of Chaos (Tiamat), The Great Father (Apsu), the hero (Marduk), and the adversary (Kingu).
- The gods agree that Marduk can be top god if he goes out and fights Tiamat—a narrative representation of the shift from polytheism towards monotheism.
- Marduk is a new god. He has four eyes, four ears, and can speak magic words, which means that he can *really* pay attention and do remarkable things with his speech.
- Marduk confronts Tiamat, traps her in a net, fills her with wind, and kills her with an arrow. After Tiamat is dead, Marduk cuts her up into pieces and uses those pieces to make the world.
- Marduk declares that the purpose of man is to eternally transform chaos into order.
- The Mesopotamian emperor was considered sovereign because he embodied Marduk.
- The Enuma elish is a Mesopotamian hypothesis about what set of attributes should be regarded as sovereign. They believed that if we paid attention and confronted the chaos in our lives with truthful speech, then we could transform that chaos into habitable order.

# CHAPTER ELEVEN

# The Myth of Osiris

ANCIENT EGYPT IS NOT ONLY one of the oldest civilizations known to man, but it was also one of the longest lasting. In fact, there is less time between Cleopatra and modern day than there is between Cleopatra and when the Egyptian pyramids were first built.[201] Let that sink in for a moment. Ancient Egypt was *old*—it was a major civilization that lasted for thousands of years, and any civilization that can last that long must have been doing something right.

Like Mesopotamia, ancient Egypt was also propped up by a set of values that can be found within the stories that they told to one another. And one of the most influential stories of this ancient civilization is commonly referred to as *the myth of Osiris*; a story which, like the Enuma elish, has contributed to the development of ideas that can be found within our own culture.

## The Myth of Osiris

Legend has it there was once an Egyptian god named Osiris, and while he was in the prime of his life, Osiris was a great hero; he founded the Egyptian state and ruled over his kingdom with fairness and benevolence. For the Egyptians, Osiris was the Wise King; he was the beneficial aspect of culture and the supportive element of tradition. But as time went on, this once great and powerful king began to grow old, tired, and set in his ways, as all traditions tend to do. And once Osiris had lost his edge, he allowed himself to become willfully blind to the problems that threatened his kingdom—that is, he began to lie to himself about how he was experiencing the world in order to avoid his responsibility of setting things right.

For starters, the deterioration of Osiris is partly a problem of entropy. Things get old and deteriorate over time, that's just a fact of life and our traditions are no different. But the deterioration that Osiris faces as a result of his old age pales in comparison to the deterioration he faces as a result of his willful blindness—which is simply to say, ignoring our problems won't make them go away, it will only cause them to get worse.

> **"For example, if you get a warning message from the tax department, the probability that ignoring it will make it go away is zero, right? What will happen instead is the more you ignore it, the larger it will grow. And if you ignore it long enough, then it will turn into something large enough to eat you. And that will be the end of you."[202]**

It is *this* kind of deterioration—the deterioration that comes as a result of willful blindness—that eventually causes the downfall of Osiris.

As the story progresses, we come to find that Osiris has an evil brother named Set—a name which later on becomes *Satan* through the Coptic Christians[203]—and Set is planning to overthrow his brother, Osiris, the first chance he gets so that he can take the kingdom for himself.

In many ways, *The Lion King* is a retelling of this ancient story. Mufasa is Osiris, Wise King and ruler of the Pride Lands, while Scar is his evil brother, Set. Like Osiris, Mufasa chooses to ignore the dangers that threaten his kingdom—that is, he chooses to ignore the dangers that are primarily related to his evil brother, Scar. At one point, Mufasa even decides to confront Scar about his recent sulking, a conversation which ends with Scar blowing him off and walking away. An angry Mufasa calls after him, "Don't turn your back on me, Scar!" To which Scar ominously replies, "Oh no, Mufasa. Perhaps *you* shouldn't turn your back on *me*." This response should have alarmed Mufasa; it should have been a wake-up call to the fact that his brother was up to no good. But unfortunately,

Mufasa chalks it up to Scar just being Scar. He chooses to not see the problem that is right in front of him and ignores his brother's resentful attitude and ominous threats. And because Mufasa, like Osiris, had no desire to see his evil brother's intentions, he was not prepared for what was to come.

Set bides his time and plays it cool until one day he catches Osiris distracted and not paying attention. Taking advantage of this opportunity, Set sneaks up on Osiris, chops him up into pieces, and scatters those pieces all over Egypt so that Osiris cannot put himself back together again. And now, with the Wise King out of the picture, the Tyrannical Father, Set, takes the throne for himself and immediately turns the kingdom of Osiris into a desolate wasteland.

This shift from the Wise King to the Tyrannical Father—from the beneficial aspect of culture to the destructive—illustrates that the only thing required for the Evil Tyrant to gain control of the kingdom is for the wise part of culture to turn a blind eye.[204] That is, if we do not pay attention and update our traditions accordingly, then they will become too old, stale, and weak to stand against the evils of tyranny.

Once again, we find that as the protective walls of culture fall, chaos ensues. Upon hearing the news of Osiris' death, his wife, Isis—queen of the underworld and creative aspect of the unknown—emerges from the underworld and travels all over Egypt looking for the pieces of her husband. And after much searching, Isis eventually finds the phallus of Osiris, uses it to impregnate herself—which means that when things fall apart and chaos reigns, the seeds of new things are also planted[205]—and descends back into the underworld to give birth to the hero of our story, Horus.

Like the Mesopotamians, the Egyptians were trying to figure something out. They wanted to know which qualities should be valued most—that is, which qualities should be given the status of "top god." And interestingly enough, it appears the Egyptians came to the same conclusion as the Mesopotamians. They believed that one of the most important qualities for making life better was our ability to pay attention—that is, having the courage to acknowledge the truth and not hide our eyes from the problems we know need fixing. This explains why Horus, the hero of Egyptian mythology, is depicted as a Falcon—a bird of prey that can *really* see[206]—and is also symbolically represented by the Egyptians as an eye (commonly referred to as the *Eye of Horus*—**see Fig. 11.1 and Fig. 11.2**).[207]

As heroes typically do, Horus grows up outside of the kingdom—remember, humble beginnings are usually a reference to the hero's humility, an idea we also see being played out with Simba growing up in the jungle, Aladdin hustling the streets of Agrabah for a loaf of bread, and Harry Potter being forced by his muggle family to live in a cupboard under the stairs. And once Horus grows up, he decides to leave home and reclaim his rightful place as king by challenging his evil uncle, Set, to a fight.

As Horus and Set battle it out for the right to be called king, they appear pretty evenly matched. At one point, Set even gains the upper hand by tearing out one of Horus' eyes,[208] as malevolence can still damage those who are courageous enough to face it. And after a couple of close calls, Horus eventually defeats Set and banishes him to the nether regions of the kingdom.[209] But it is what Horus does next, that really deserves our attention:

> Horus recovers his eye. A sensible person, in such a situation, would thank his lucky stars, place the eye back into its empty socket, and get on with his life. But that is not what Horus does. He returns, instead, to the underworld, to the belly of the beast, to the kingdom of the dead, where he knows he will find the spirit of Osiris. Dismembered though he may be, near death—even dead, in a sense—Osiris inhabits the underworld domain of chaos itself. That is the dead father in the belly of the beast. Horus finds the once-great king and grants to him the eye torn out by Set. Once again—because of the sacrifice and vision of his son—the ancient of days can see. Horus then takes his father, vision restored, and returns with him to the kingdom, so they can rule in tandem. The Egyptians insisted that it was this combination of vision, courage, and regenerated tradition that constituted the proper sovereign of the kingdom.[210]

This is an incredible addition to the hero story by the Egyptians. They understood that the hero not only confronts chaos and makes

Figure 11.1

Figure 11.2

the world out of her pieces, but he also rescues order when it has lost its way.[211] They believed that the hero is he who voluntarily journey's to the underworld and rescues his father from destruction; he who gives blind tradition sight, knowing that he will need his tradition in order to to rule the kingdom properly.

All cultures grow old and eventually become stale and outdated. But when this happens what should we do? We can't just throw our traditions away because if we do, as the Mesopotamians have pointed out, Tiamat will make it point to pay us a visit.[212] Instead, as the Egyptians have so brilliantly illustrated in the myth of Osiris, *it is up to us to pay attention and revive our traditions whenever we see that they are lagging behind.* And if this is done properly, then we will be able to keep our culture from self-destructing or falling into the hands of tyranny.[213]

This story—the story of the hero who rescues his father from the underworld—is a story that has been so fundamental to the development of our own culture that most of us are probably already familiar with some version of it. Take *Pinocchio*, for example. Near the end of the movie *Pinocchio*, Pinocchio tries to return home to his father, Geppetto (the Wise Old Man), only to find that he is no longer there. This is a shock to Pinocchio, and he doesn't know what to do until the Blue Fairy (the beneficial aspect of the unknown) informs him that Geppetto has been swallowed by a terrifying whale named Monstro (the Dragon of Chaos) who lives at the bottom of the sea (the underworld).[214] Upon hearing this, Pinocchio decides to courageously journey to the underworld and rescue his father from this monster.

After much searching, Pinocchio eventually finds Monstro at the bottom of the sea and ends up sacrificing his life in order to save his father from captivity. And as a dead Pinocchio lays next to a grieving Geppetto, we hear the voice of the Blue Fairy, *"Prove yourself brave, truthful, and unselfish, and someday you will be a real boy. Awake, Pinocchio. Awake."* Miraculously, Pinocchio resurrects from the dead, except with one important distinction—he is no longer a puppet but a real boy!

We will never become true individuals until we let the puppet within ourselves die—that is, until we interact with our experiences truthfully and refuse to blindly follow the crowd.[215]

As Jean Piaget pointed out, there is much more to us than we consciously understand; we are currently acting out ideas that have their roots deep within our historical past, and these ideas have helped shape who we are to our very core. Therefore, if we truly want to understand who we are and why we are here, then we must first understand our past and the traditions it has produced—that is, we must rescue our father from the underworld, from the belly of the beast; we must give our father sight and lead him back to the land of the living. Only then, when we are grounded within the historical past of mankind, will it be possible for us to become true individuals, as opposed to puppets, and live in a kingdom that flourishes.

Once again, this is an idea that can also be found more subtly in *The Lion King*. As Simba grows up outside of his kingdom, he falls into the trap of allowing others to control him like a puppet—he refuses to interact truthfully with his own experience as a lion, and as a result has resorted to eating bugs, as well as doing other things that are unnatural for lions to be doing. One night, Simba runs into a baboon named Rafiki, and as they talk, Simba realizes that Rafiki was actually an old friend of his father, Mufasa.

"You knew my father?" Simba asks.

"Correction—I *know* your father."

This dampens Simba's spirits. "I hate to tell you this, but he died a long time ago."

Rafiki jumps to his feet and exclaims, "Nope! Wrong again! Ha Ha Ha! He's *alive*! I'll show him to you! You follow 'ole Rafiki, he knows the way!"

At that, Rafiki takes off running into a dark, nearby forest—the domain of the underworld—with a confused Simba hot on his heels. After a deep descent into the forest, Rafiki stops next to a calm pool of water.

"Look down there," Rafiki says, gesturing towards the water.

Cautiously, Simba approaches the pool of water and gazes down.

"That's not my father. That's just my reflection." Simba sadly informs Rafiki.

Delicately placing his hand on Simba, Rafiki points back to the water and says, "No, look harder."

At this, Simba slowly looks back down and gazes into the water, where he begins to see his father, Mufasa, take shape within his own reflection.

"You see?" Rafiki continues, "*He lives in you.*"

And as soon as Simba sees his father within himself, the heavens open up and an apparition of Mufasa appears in the clouds and speaks.

"Simba, you have forgotten me. You have forgotten who you are, and so you have forgotten me. Look inside yourself, Simba. You are more than what you have become. You must take your place in the circle of life."

"How can I go back? I'm not who I use to be." Simba asks his father.

As his ghost retreats back into the clouds, Mufasa responds, "Remember who you are. You are my son, and the one true king. Remember who you are."

*The Lion King* has Simba descending deep into the underworld in order to rescue the father that lies dormant within himself. And as a result of this encounter—as a result of remembering and reviving his dead tradition—Simba finds the strength and direction he needs to return home and defeat his evil uncle, Scar, and save his kingdom from destruction.

Like the Enuma elish, the myth of Osiris is an attempt by the Egyptians to figure out what should be regarded as sovereign. And ultimately, they came to the conclusion that it was the combination of Horus and Osiris—the combination of paying attention and renewed tradition—that would save the world from destruction. And just like the Mesopotamians, the Egyptians associated this sovereignty with their leader because he was the one who embodied this Horus/Osiris combination.[216] But as time progressed, the idea of sovereignty—the idea of having an immortal soul—was something that was eventually passed down through the social hierarchy of man. It was first something attributed to the pharaoh, but over time it was used to describe the entire Egyptian aristocracy. And then by the time the Greeks came along, the concept of a divine soul was something that was only attributed to those who were a part of the political structure. And it was the Christians, lastly, who took the idea of sovereignty and attributed it to everyone—men, women, slaves, prostitutes, tax collectors, murderers, *everyone*.[217] The Christians believed that everyone had the ability to embody the hero and therefore should be treated as having intrinsic value. And it was the idea of the sovereign individual—the idea that there is a relationship between the individual and something that is divine—that served as the bedrock upon which the entirety of Western civilization was founded.

*"We hold these truths to be self-evident, that all men are created equal, that they are endowed by their Creator with certain unalienable Rights . . ."*

–The Declaration of Independence

The idea of natural rights in the United States is based on the idea of sovereignty—the idea that every individual can be the hero; that every individual, like Marduk and Horus, has the ability to transform chaos into order, as well as revive their dead culture. And this divine spark within each of us is to be respected so much that even if we witness someone committing the worst of crimes, we still have to act as if their life is intrinsically valuable and provide them with due process.[218]

Near the end of the nineteenth century, Nietzsche announced that God was dead. But perhaps He's not. Perhaps, like Osiris, He is only languishing away in the underworld, blind, waiting for his sons to restore his sight. We struggle to find purpose in a world with no meaning and have carelessly thrown out our past traditions under the delusion that they have nothing to offer us. But unfortunately, our traditions are not something we can throw away without consequences. Just because the traditions of our culture do not fit nicely within a scientific framework does not mean they are wrong, it just means we need to update how we think about them; it means we need to make them relevant again by journeying to the underworld and rescuing our father from the belly of the beast. And if we are successful in doing this, then perhaps these traditions can provide us with the wisdom and direction we need to rediscover the meaning and purpose of our lives.

## Recap

- Ancient Egypt is not only one of the oldest civilizations known to man, but it was also one of the longest lasting.

- One of the most influential stories of this ancient civilization is called the *myth of Osiris*, a story that has also shaped the values and ideas of our own culture.
- Osiris is the Wise King who has become old and willfully blind to the things that threaten his kingdom.
- The Egyptian hero, Horus, represents the ability to pay attention.
- Horus takes the eye that Set has torn out, descends into the underworld, and gives it to his father, Osiris. They then rise back up and rule together.
- The Myth of Osiris is an ancient Egyptian hypothesis about what set of attributes should be regarded as sovereign. They believed that the hero not only pays attention and transforms chaos into order, but that he also revives his dead culture.
- The Egyptian pharaoh was the only one who was considered sovereign, because he embodied the combination of Horus and Osiris. But over time, the idea of sovereignty was eventually passed down through the social hierarchy of man and attributed to everyone.

# Part Two Recap

## The Foundation of Mythology

Ancient stories are not scientific descriptions of the world, they are stories about how we should act within the world of meaning. The world of meaning is made up of explored and unexplored territory, two conceptual places that our brains have evolved to navigate within. Now. if evolution is defined as "the body adapting to reality," and if our brains have evolved to represent explored and unexplored territory, then that means these two conceptual places can be considered a fundamental reality. To realize this is to realize that there is a reality that exists outside of the material world. Our ancestors observed the fundamental patterns of existence, and then expressed these patterns as characters in a story.

## The Players of Mythology - Part One

The characters of mythology are a result of our ancestors using social categories—mother, father, child (individual), predator—to understand a personified world. The precosmogonic chaos is the field of potential that gives rise to everything and is represented in mythology as the Dragon of Chaos, the ultimate predator who guards something of value. Unexplored territory is represented in mythology as chaos and is portrayed by the Great Mother. The Creative Mother is the beneficial aspect of chaos, and the Destructive Mother is the destructive aspect. Explored territory is represented in mythology as order and is portrayed by the Great Father. The Protective Father is the beneficial aspect of order, and the Tyrannical Father is the destructive aspect.

## The Players of Mythology - Part Two

The individual has both a positive and negative aspect and therefore is represented in mythology by two characters: the hero and the adversary. The hero pursues redemptive knowledge—*truth*—above all things, and attempts to make things better. He is a collection of attitudes and actions that work, and his character arc—the hero's journey—illustrates the fundamental story of mankind. The adversary is the destructive aspect of the individual who rejects truth in favor of the lie; he feels cheated by life, and as a result of stewing in his resentment, attempts to make things worse instead of better.

## The Enuma Elish

Marduk is the hero of the Mesopotamian creation myth and represents what the Mesopotamians believed were the most important qualities for turning chaos into order—*attention and truthful speech*. Also, the Enuma elish claims that mankind was created for a purpose: to eternally transform chaos into order.

## The Myth of Osiris

Horus is the hero of Egyptian mythology and represents the Egyptian hypothesis of what should be regarded as sovereign. The Egyptians believed that the hero not only transforms chaos into order, but that he also revives the dead traditions of his culture.

# Part
# Three

CHAPTER TWELVE

# In the Beginning

IN THE BEGINNING, WE WERE creatures acting in the world according to our nature. But as time progressed, we began to wake up; we began to watch ourselves act, and told stories about how we were acting, stories which were then passed down and perfected by many different people over thousands of years. Eventually, these stories were collected and placed into an order that miraculously made some sort of narrative sense. And together, this collection of stories makes up what is now known as *The Holy Bible*, a book that sits at the bottom of our culture and has deeply influenced the world we live in today.[219]

The Bible is a book about us; it is a collaborative effort by mankind to figure out who we are, where we came from, and where we should be going. It is a book that contains the unconscious wisdom of our species; wisdom that, if properly understood, may help us rediscover the purpose of our lives.

## In the Beginning

In the beginning God created the heavens and the earth. Now the earth was formless and empty, darkness was over the surface of the deep, and the Spirit of God was hovering over the waters. . . .

And God said, "Let there be an expanse between the waters to separate water from water." So God made the expanse and separated the water under the expanse from the water above it. And it was so. God called the expanse "sky." And there was evening, and there was morning . . .

And God said, "Let the water under the sky be gathered to one place, and let dry ground appear." And it was so. God called the dry ground "land," and the gathered waters he called "seas." And God saw that it was good. (Genesis 1:1-10)

In the first book of the Bible, God creates the heavens and the earth by separating the two waters that existed before time began, an idea that we are already somewhat familiar with from our study of the *Enuma elish*. Remember, in the beginning of the Mesopotamian creation myth there is also an intermingling of two primordial waters, Apsu and Tiamat—the totality from which all things emerge. Now what's interesting about this is, when Genesis 1:2 states that "darkness was over the surface of the deep," the Hebrew word used for "the deep" is *tehom*, and it is a word that is derived from the Sumerian word *Tiamat*, the Dragon of Chaos herself.[220] Therefore, it can be inferred that the chaos God uses to make the heavens and the earth in Genesis is the same chaos that Marduk uses to create the heavens and the earth in the Enuma elish, an idea that is further elaborated on in the book of Job when God recounts to Job His battle with the leviathan, a serpent of the sea:

Can you pull in the leviathan with a fishhook or tie down its tongue with a rope?

Can you put a cord though his nose or pierce his jaw with a hook?

Will he keep begging you for mercy? Will he speak to you with gentle words? . . .

Will he make an agreement with you for you to take him as your slave for life?

Can you make a pet of him like a bird or put him on a leash for your girls?

Will traders barter for him? Will they divide him up among the merchants?

Can you fill his hide with harpoons or his head with fishing spears?

If you lay a hand on him, you will remember the struggle and never do it again!

Any hope of subduing him is false; the mere sight of him is overpowering.

No one is fierce enough to rouse him. Who then is able to stand against me?

Who has a claim against me that I must pay? Everything under heaven belongs to me.

I will not fail to speak of his limbs, his strength and his graceful form.

Who can strip off his outer coat? Who would approach him with a bridle?

Who dares open the doors of his mouth, ringed about with his fearsome teeth?

His back has rows of shields tightly sealed together; each is so close to the next that no air can pass between.

They are joined fast to one another; they cling together and cannot be parted.

His snorting throws out flashes of light; his eyes are like the rays of dawn.

*Firebrands stream from his mouth; sparks of fire shoot out.*

*Smoke pours from his nostrils as from a boiling pot over a fire of reeds.*

*His breath sets coals ablaze, and flames dart from his mouth.*

Strength resides in his neck; dismay goes before him.

The folds of his flesh are tightly joined; they are firm and immovable.

His chest is hard as rock, hard as a lower millstone.

When he rises up, the mighty are terrified; they retreat before his thrashing.

The sword that reaches him has no effect, nor does the spear or the dart or the javelin.

Iron he treats like straw and bronze like rotten wood.

Arrows do not make him flee; clingstones relive chaff to him.

A club seems to him but a piece of straw; he laughs at the rattling of the lance.

His undersides are jagged potsherds, leaving a trail in the mud like a threshing sledge.

He makes the depths churn like a boiling caldron and stirs up
the sea like a pot of ointment.
Behind him he leaves a glistening wake; one would think the
deep had white hair.
Nothing on earth is his equal—a creature without fear.
He looks down on all that are haughty; he is king over all
that are proud.
(Job 41:1–34; bold and italics added)

**"So what's God doing here? He's describing what He defeated
in order to create the world.** *That's Marduk and Tiamat!*
**That's one reference like that. Here's another reference like
that—this is from Psalms 74:**

> **'Thou didst break the sea in pieces by thy strength.
> Thou didst shatter the heads of the sea monsters in
> the waters. Thou did crush the heads of Leviathan.
> Thou gavest him to be food to the folk inhabiting
> the wilderness.'**

**"Now you remember, when Marduk defeats Tiamat, he cuts her
into pieces and makes the world out of her pieces. And here
what's happening is the force that encounters the Leviathan
is able to break it into pieces and feed everyone with it. . . .**

**"So the idea that's presented at the beginning of Gen-
esis is an abstracted and psychologized representation of
the story that the Mesopotamians put forward. Yahweh
is Marduk, roughly speaking, going out and conquering
the Dragon of Chaos and making order out of it. Then
there are these allusions later in Job and Psalms of Him
doing exactly that—conquering a primordial monster and
making the world out of its pieces. And so what does that
mean exactly? It means that the highest ordering principle
is the spirit that goes out into the darkness (or the deep),
encounters the Dragon of Chaos—because obviously the
leviathan is a dragon—defeats it, and feeds the people as
a consequence."[221]**

In the beginning of Genesis, God, like Marduk, speaks the world into existence; He confronts the chaos that existed before time began and uses his speech to create the world out of that chaos. Now in the Christian tradition, the speech God uses to create the heavens and the earth is referred to as the *logos*, something which can be thought of as *truthful speech aimed at making things better*, or said another way, *truthful speech motivated by love*. And it is this kind of speech—truthful speech motivated by love—that even God himself credits for bringing about good things. In fact, every time God creates something using the logos, Genesis makes it a point to tell the reader, "And God saw that it was good."[222]

The idea that everything brought into the world by the logos is good, regardless of what it is,[223] is an idea that we find strengthened by the philosophies of our time. Sigmund Freud believed that mental illness could be associated with repression (avoidance of truth), Carl Rogers believed that truthful dialogue between two people was curative, and the existentialists thought that hell on earth could be avoided if individuals would only speak the truth and refuse to falsify their own experiences. It is the logos—the truth—that creates good things and saves the world from disaster. And it is the logos that God uses in the beginning of Genesis to create order out of chaos.

And once God had finished creating the heavens and the earth, He then decides to make man:

Then God said, "Let us make man in our image, in our likeness …"

So God created man in his own image,
    in the image of God he created him;
    male and female he created them. (Genesis 1:26–27)

Now what does it mean that God made man in his own likeness? Well, at this point in the story, what do we know about God? We know that God uses the logos to create good things out of chaos. And so, if man and woman are created in the *likeness* of God, then that means we also can use the logos to create good things out of chaos. As humans, we have the unique ability to envision certain futures and then work to bring those futures about; we have the ability to turn potential into actuality, *to turn chaos into order*, and it is this ability that Genesis associates with the divine likeness of God and then grants to all of mankind.

The logos is the mechanism that keeps the world from falling apart. It is what allows us to create order out of chaos, as well as defend against the tyranny of order. The logos—the truth motivated by love—is what God uses to face the leviathan, separate the primordial waters, and create the cosmos at the beginning of time. And it is the logos that God gifts to mankind in the beginning of Genesis.

## Adam and Eve

> God blessed them and said to them, "Be fruitful and increase in number; fill the earth and subdue it. Rule over the fish of the sea and the birds of the air and over every living creature that moves on the ground. . . ."
>
> Now the LORD God had planted a garden in the east, in Eden; and there he put the man he had formed. And the LORD God made all kinds of trees grow out of the ground—trees that were pleasing to the eye and good for food. In the middle of the garden were the tree of life and the tree of the knowledge of good and evil. . . .
>
> The LORD God took the man and put him in the Garden of Eden to work it and take care of it. And the LORD God commanded the man, "You are free to eat from any tree in the garden; but you must not eat from the tree of the knowledge of good and evil, for when you eat of it you will surely die."
> (Genesis 1:28; 2:8-9,15–17)

Once God finished creating the world, He took a step back and saw that it was good. But "good" doesn't mean "perfect," nor does it mean "final." And so as God was looking over what He had created, He saw there was still work that needed to be done and, therefore, created man and woman to continue what He had started. Like Marduk, God created mankind and gave them the responsibility of transforming chaos into order; He created them for the purpose of making things better by furthering his creation, and in doing so, gave them the authority to cultivate the earth and shape it into something that produced good things.

And once mankind was created, God then placed them into a beautiful garden and instructed them to take care of it. But this was no ordinary garden—in the middle of this garden grew the tree of the knowledge of good and evil, a tree that God commanded mankind to not eat from, for if they did, they would surely die.

Soon after God leaves man alone to tend the garden, a serpent—the predatory aspect of chaos—approaches the woman, Eve—the feminine source from which all new things emerge—and innocently asks something like, "Did God *really* say you cannot eat from any tree in the garden?"[224] Which is more like asking, "Is God *really* that ridiculous and unfair?" Caught off guard, Eve quickly replies, "We can too eat from any tree in the garden, just not from the tree of the knowledge of good and evil—if we eat from *that* tree, God says we will surely die."[225] Seeing his chance, and having already planted the seed of doubt in Eve's mind about the fairness of God, the serpent responds with something along the lines of, "What?! You will not surely die! God only said that because He knows once you eat from it your eyes will be opened and you will be just like Him knowing good and evil."[226] This gets Eve thinking. . . .

> When the woman saw that the fruit of the tree was good for food and pleasing to the eye, and also desirable for gaining wisdom, she took some and ate it. She also gave some to her husband, who was with her, and he ate it. Then the eyes of both of them were opened, and they realized they were naked. (Genesis 3:6–7)

Deep down, Eve knew that she shouldn't eat from this mysterious tree, but once she saw that its fruit was pleasing to the eye, she chose to eat from it anyway. In a moment of weakness, Eve placed her own selfish desires above what she knew to be right, her own pleasure above her commitment to the truth, and her divinely appointed duty to make things better. And once she had finished eating from this forbidden tree, she then gave some of its fruit to her puppet of a husband, Adam, who quickly followed suit.

According to the Christian tradition, this is the moment when sin first entered into the world. Now the word *sin* is often translated from the Greek word *hamartia*, a word that was originally an archery term meaning *to miss the mark or target*.[227] And so "to sin" means *to miss the mark*; it means to fall short in our commitment to the truth, to place our own selfish desires above what we know to be right and, therefore, to avoid the responsibility we have in making things better.

Now, before Adam and Eve ate from the tree of the knowledge of good and evil, Genesis 2:25 says that they were "naked and unashamed." Yet, after eating from this forbidden tree, we learn that their eyes were opened, and that they realized they were naked. This begs the question: what does realizing we are naked have to do with obtaining the knowledge of good and evil?

For starters, remember that our ancestors began by acting in the world first; essentially, they were animals existing in a paradisal state of unawareness; or said another way, their eyes were closed and they were unashamed of their nakedness. But as time progressed and we began to become more self-conscious, we started to understand that we were vulnerable and could be hurt. In fact, that is actually what it means to realize that we are naked—it is to become all too aware of our own inadequacies and vulnerabilities.

The discovery that we were naked—that we were inadequate and vulnerable—in many ways, was also the discovery of time itself; when we became self-conscious, we discovered the future and the fact that even if we were not hungry, sick, or old right now, we inevitably would be at some point down the road. And as a result of discovering the future, we also learned that one day we would surely die. And it was this massive event in history—the dawn of consciousness—that the Christians refer to as *the fall of man*.[228]

**"It's a radical transformation! You might say that it's good because lions don't eat us as often—it's like, yeah, the zebras don't seem that upset on the plains of the Serengeti when the lions are around. One is going to get picked off every now and then, but the zebras aren't running around with anxiety disorders popping valium all the time because the lions are**

**there. But that's not the case with human beings. We see a
lion and think, 'At some point, that lion is going to eat one
of us. . . .' And so we not only have to solve the problem of
that lion right now, but we also have to solve the problem
of all lions for all time."²²⁹**

As a species, once we became conscious and saw that we were
vulnerable, we instantly understood all the different ways that we
could be hurt. And once we understood how we could be hurt, we
also understood how we could hurt other people; we learned how we
could cause other people large amounts of unnecessary pain, and also
how we could turn that pain into a sadistic game. Thus, through the
dawn of consciousness, the knowledge of good and evil also entered
into the world.²³⁰

And as if on cue, as soon as Adam and Eve finish eating from
the forbidden tree, they hear God walking along in the garden calling
their names:

> Then the man and his wife heard the sound of the LORD God
> as he was walking in the garden in the cool of the day, and they
> hid from the LORD God among the trees of the garden. But
> the LORD God called to the man, "Where are you?"
>
> He answered, "I heard you in the garden, and I was afraid
> because I was naked; so I hid."
>
> And he said, "Who told you that you were naked? Have
> you eaten from the tree that I commanded you not to eat
> from?" (Genesis 3:8–11)

**"I think this part of the story is actually a comedy because
Adam and Eve are really acting in a brainless manner. It's like,
first of all, *they're hiding from God behind trees?* It strikes me
that that's a pretty ineffective way of hiding from God since
he can probably see through trees.²³¹ So God says, 'Where
have you gone?' And Adam says, 'I'm hiding' . . . God says,
'Why are you hiding?' It's because Adam is ashamed—Adam
says, 'I'm naked.' And this is an example of the tremendous compression of human wisdom into a few lines that**

**characterizes mythology. Why would people hide from God
once they realize they're naked?"[232]**

So far, we know that God is something which transforms chaos
into order using the logos. We also know that God made man in
His own likeness. And so, whenever we successfully embody the
logos—that is, whenever we live courageously, truthfully, and strive
to make things better using our speech and actions—it could be
said that we are embodying the essence and likeness of God and
therefore walking with God in the garden. But once we realize that
we are naked and imperfect, we have an inclination to hide from
God. We look at ourselves and think, "How in the world could I
make anything better, given how completely flawed I am? How
could I possibly have courage or live in truth, given my complete
and utter inadequacy?"[233] When we realize that we are naked, we
realize that we are ultimately flawed and vulnerable. And so, out of
fear of being hurt and judged, we hide from our responsibility to
embody the logos and make things better—that is, we hide from
God and shrink away from the best in ourselves.[234] And *that* is
what this story tells us—that when humans woke up and became
self-conscious, they immediately realized they were vulnerable and
inadequate, and that realization caused them to hide from their
purpose and "manifesting their divine destiny."[235]

Caught red-handed, Adam and Eve confess to God what they
have done, and in response, God tells them what will come as result.

> To the woman he said, "I will greatly increase your pains in
> childbearing; with pain you will give birth to children. Your
> desire will be for your husband, and he will rule over you."
>
> To Adam he said, "Because you listened to your wife and
> ate from the tree about which I commanded you, 'You must not
> eat of it,' cursed is the ground because of you; through painful
> toil you will eat of it all the days of your life. It will produce
> thorns and thistles for you, and you will eat the plants of the
> field. By the sweat of your brow you will eat your food until
> you return to the ground, since from it you were taken; for
> dust you are and to dust you will return." (Genesis 3:16–19)

"A sequence of events has just occurred as a result of the emergence of self-consciousness. Now we can assume the emergence of self-consciousness was associated with cortical expansion. One of the things we know that happened during cortical expansion was that babies heads got so damn big that they couldn't get out during childbirth. And there's been a bunch of physiological consequences of that, one of which is women's hips are wider than men's—if they were any wider, then women wouldn't be able to run! So women hit the limits of hip expansion. And hip expansion helped make the pelvic gap through which the baby is born sufficiently large so that the baby's head could get through, but barely. Like seriously, barely. . . .

"Birth is very, very painful for human beings, and it's very, very dangerous . . . Human babies are unbelievably vulnerable. Even at birth they're highly likely to die. Child mortality has been a terrible burden on humanity really up until the last century . . . Prior to the twentieth century, the majority of children died. Women died in childbirth all the time, so the idea that women were going to have sorrow in childbirth doesn't seem to me to be precisely a divine doctrine, it's just an observation of exactly what was going to happen.

"And then once the baby is born, the baby is so premature and so helpless that the woman is basically doomed to be non-self-sufficient for a reasonably extensive period of time—we could say until the baby is five, absolutely minimum . . . Human mothers are at a tremendous disadvantage in the immediate aftermath of birth, and part of the consequence of that is they're doomed to be reliant on men. What the hell else could possibly happen? . . . It's a statement of destiny rather than a sentence of revenge."[236]

Then God turns to Adam and says that because he is now aware of the future, he is going to have to work for the rest of his life in order to protect his family from that future. And with that, God banishes both Adam and Eve from the Garden of Eden out into the real world where they must struggle and work for the rest of their lives. And it is here where the story of the Bible truly begins, a story that depicts man's attempt to find his way back to paradise so that he may walk with God in the garden once more.

## Recap

- The Bible is a collection of books that rests at the very bottom of our culture and has shaped the world we live in today. It is a collection of books that are rooted in our behavior, authored by many different people, passed down and perfected over thousands of years, and placed into an order that makes some sort of narrative sense.
- God created the world out of chaos using the logos, *truthful speech aimed at making things better*, or said another way, *truthful speech motivated by love*.
- God created man in His own likeness, which means that men and women also have the ability to create order out of chaos using the logos.
- God created man for a purpose: to make things better by furthering His creation.
- Man chose not to trust in God, chose not to have faith. This resulted in him placing his own selfish desires above what he knew to be right and eating from the forbidden tree, an act which ultimately caused his downfall.
- Upon realizing they were naked, Adam and Eve hid from God and therefore turned away from their responsibility of making things better.
- As a result of their sin, God banished man from the garden, and the rest of the Bible is an account of man's attempt to find his way back.

# CHAPTER THIRTEEN

# East of Eden

## Cain and Abel

AFTER BEING BANISHED FROM THE garden of Eden, Adam and Even make their way out into the real world where Eve eventually gives birth to two sons, Cain and Abel. And once Cain and Abel are old enough to work, they begin making sacrifices to God in hopes that He will be pleased and grant them good fortune.[237]

Now, it's easy to fall into the trap of thinking that making sacrifices to God is primitive and superstitious. But that's just not the case. In fact, sacrifice may be one of the most sophisticated ideas mankind has ever come up with. Fundamentally, the ritual act of sacrifice is nothing more than a dramatic representation of the idea of delayed gratification. It is the realization that we can protect ourselves from future suffering by giving up something that we value in the present, that we can sacrifice momentary pleasure for the possibility of future gain.

Our ancestors acted out a drama, a fiction: they personified the force that governs fate as a spirit that can be bargained with, traded with, as if it were another human being. And the amazing thing is *that it worked*. This was in part because the future is largely composed of other human beings—often precisely those who have watched and evaluated and appraised the tiniest details of your past behavior. It's not very far from that to God, sitting above on high, tracking your every move and writing it down for further reference in a big book. Here's a productive symbolic idea: *the future is a judgmental father.* That's a good start.[238]

Sacrifice is mankind's hypothesis on how to minimize future suffering, which might account for why this story comes immediately after the fall in Genesis.[239] As humans, we are constantly making sacrifices; we assume that if we sacrifice our time, among other things, in the pursuit of some task—say, a medical degree—then our sacrifices will be honored in the future in the form of certain opportunities that otherwise would not have been possible.[240] And although we understand this idea in an articulated way and can say things like "delayed gratification," this concept wasn't always so clear. As a species, we didn't just wake up one day and say, "I just discovered time! I guess that means I should start delaying my gratification!" No. This idea took a *very* long time to develop. It was an idea that we acted out first, an idea that we understood in an embodied way long before we could understand it explicitly. And as we continued to make sacrifices, we began to represent how we were behaving in the form of dramatic rituals—*sacrificial* dramatic rituals—and from there, it was only a matter of time before we began telling stories about the rituals that we found ourselves performing.

> In the course of time Cain brought some of the fruits of the soil as an offering to the LORD. But Abel brought fat portions from some of the firstborn of his flock. The LORD looked with favor on Abel and his offering, but on Cain and his offering he did not look with favor. So Cain was very angry, and his face was downcast.
> Then the LORD said to Cain, "Why are you angry? Why is your face downcast? If you do what is right, will you not be accepted? But if you do not do what is right, sin is crouching at your door; it desires to have you, but you must master it." (Genesis 4:3–7)

When offering his sacrifice to God, Abel puts his best foot forward; he does the best that he can with what he has, and as a result,

God looks upon him with favor. Essentially, this means that things are working out well for Abel; he has made the proper sacrifices and, therefore, his relationships are flourishing, his flocks are increasing, and it seems like everything he touches turns to gold.[241]

But Cain, on the other hand, is not as fortunate as his brother Abel. When offering *his* sacrifice to God, it appears that Cain does not do his best, and therefore God disapproves of his offering. Ultimately, this means that things aren't going very well for Cain—people don't really like him all that much, and it's as if everything he does results in failure, especially in comparison to his brother Abel, who it seems can do no wrong. And as a result of constantly feeling like life has dealt him a bad hand, Cain quickly grows angry, resentful, and jealous of his brother.[242]

"It's not difficult to understand that. You know perfectly well what happens when you think that you are working hard but nothing is going your way, all the while some other son of a bitch is just flourishing like mad beside of you. That's going to make you vengeful, irritated, anxious, angry, and even homicidal for that matter. And it doesn't take very long for people to reach that stage, at least not in their fantasies.

"The story says, 'And Cain was very wroth, and his countenance fell'—that means he's angry, and his face has changed to indicate that . . . So he goes and has a chat with God because things aren't going very well for him—I think people do that all the time even if they don't necessarily formulate it in those terms. It's like they're thinking, 'What's the nature of reality? I'm busting myself in half trying to make things work properly, and nothing is going well. What kind of stupid universe is this?' For all intents and purposes, that's a conversation with God because you don't start thinking about the ultimate fabric of reality without bringing religious intuitions into it. You can't even ask such a question without acting in a quasi-religious manner."[243]

When things fall apart for Cain, his first impulse is to question God; he asks, "Why is this happening to me? How could you make a universe so unfair that it treats me this way?" To which God responds with something like, "What are you complaining to me for? If you would just do your best and what you knew to be right, then things would go better for you. Except you have chosen to do the things you know to be wrong."[244] This answer *really* annoys Cain. Instead of recognizing that he played a part in his own misfortune—which is actually good news because that means he could fix it—he refuses to accept the truth; he angrily looks around at the people who life has blessed and hates them for it; but even more, he hates God for setting things up in such an unfair way. And as a result of stewing in his own resentment, Cain grows to hate the world and decides to take revenge on life itself; he decides to strike back at God, as well as anything that shines a light on his failures and, therefore, takes his brother Abel out into a field and kills him.[245]

**"Cain does the ultimate thing . . . What happens is you go from 'I'm irritated because things aren't working out for me very well,' to 'I'm irritated and I hate those people for whom things are working out well,' to 'I'm irritated and I hate the fact that this is the way the world is set up so that this has happened to me.' And then you go to 'Well, because I'm irritated and hate the world, I'm going to do whatever I can to destroy it, and with the highest possible amount of pain and suffering conceivable.' And at that point, you don't just shoot up the high school, you go and shoot up the elementary school. And so if you're wondering what kind of pathway people walk down to get to that point, *that's* the pathway."[246]**

The story of Cain and Abel is not a story about two different people, it is a story about the two different ways we can respond to the tragedies of life, the two paths that lay before us in each moment of every day. You see, within each of us exists both a Cain *and* an Abel, and whichever personality we choose to embrace is ultimately up to us. When faced with the unfairness of life, the question we must ultimately ask ourselves is this: do we want to make things better, or do we want to make things worse? Do we want to be the hero or do we want to be the adversary? Do we want to be Cain, or do we want to be Abel?

Again, we see this idea represented in *Harry Potter*. Throughout the Harry Potter series we learn that Harry has a piece of Voldemort inside of him, that is, a piece of evil. And in the beginning of *Harry Potter and the Sorcerer's Stone* when the "sorting hat" is placed on Harry's head—a hat which peers into the minds of those who wear it and places them into a suitable house—we watch Harry fight with this inner darkness about being placed in the Slytherin house, a house with an evil, yet powerful reputation:

### SORTING HAT

Hmmm . . . Difficult. Very Difficult . . . Plenty of courage, I see. Not a bad mind, either. There's talent, oh yes. And a thirst to prove yourself . . . But where to put you?

### HARRY POTTER

(Closing his eyes and whispering to himself)

Not Slytherin. Not Slytherin.

### SORTING HAT

Not Slytherin, eh? Are you sure? You could be great, you know. It's all here in your head. And Slytherin will help you on the way to greatness, there's no doubt about that.

### HARRY POTTER

(Whispering harder)

No, please! Please! Anything but Slytherin! Anything but Slytherin!

### SORTING HAT

No? Well, if you're sure . . . Better be . . . Gryffindor!

There is a battle between good and evil happening inside all of us, and whichever side wins depends entirely on the choices we make. When we feel like our sacrifices have been rejected by God, how are we going to respond? Will we take ownership in the outcome of our lives, and despite feeling cheated, strive to make things better? Or will we turn our backs on God and seek revenge? In its essence, this is what it means to be human; it means to live within a landscape of morality; it means that every decision we make boils down to whether or not we are trying to make things better or make things worse; it means to choose on a daily basis between Cain or Abel—a choice which will ultimately determine the outcome of our lives, as well as the direction of the world.

> One evening an old Cherokee told his grandson about a battle that goes on inside all people . . .
>
> He said, "My son, there is a terrible battle between two wolves that exists inside us all.
>
> One is Evil. It is anger, envy, jealousy, sorrow, regret, greed, arrogance, self-pity, guilt, resentment, inferiority, lies, false pride, superiority, and ego.
>
> The other is good. It is joy, peace, love, hope, serenity, humility, kindness, benevolence, empathy, generosity, truth, compassion, and faith."
>
> The boy thought about it for a moment and then asked his grandfather, "Which wolf wins?"
>
> The old Cherokee simply replied, "The one you feed."
>
> – Author Unknown –

## The Flood

After killing his brother Abel, Cain is cursed by God and driven from the land where he eventually finds a wife and starts a family of his own.[247] Now Cain's descendants are very much like their father in that they strive to make things worse instead of better. Take Lamech, for example, a fifth generation descendent of Cain, who sings songs about murdering a man because of his own suffering and resentment.[248]

Or consider Tu-bal-Cain, a man who forges weapons of war—an indication that the attitude of Cain has spread throughout the world and is now causing violence and destruction on a mass scale.[249] These descriptions of Cain's descendants are the Bible's attempt to depict a world that has been corrupted by the attitude of Cain, a world where people are more interested in pursuing their own selfish desires than they are in doing what they know to be right. And once this fallen world has been successfully portrayed to the reader, we then learn that God has had enough and plans to destroy every living thing on the earth—that is, every living thing but one man . . . a man by the name of Noah.

> The LORD saw how great man's wickedness on the earth had become, and that every inclination of the thoughts of his heart was only evil all the time. The LORD was grieved that he had made man on the earth, and his heart was filled with pain. So the LORD said, "I will wipe mankind, whom I have created, from the face of the earth—men and animals, and creatures that move along the ground, and birds of the air—for I am grieved that I have made them." But Noah found favor in the eyes of the LORD.
>
> This is the account of Noah.
>
> Noah was a righteous man, blameless among the people of his time, and he walked with God. . . .
>
> Now the earth was corrupt in God's sight and was full of violence. God saw how corrupt the earth had become, for all the people on earth had corrupted their ways. So God said to Noah, "I am going to put an end to all people, for the earth is filled with violence because of them. I am surely going to destroy both them and the earth. So make yourself an ark of cypress wood . . . I am going to bring floodwaters on the earth to destroy all life under the heavens, every creature that has the breath of life in it. Everything on earth will perish. But I will establish my covenant with you, and you will enter the ark—you and your sons and your wife and your sons' wives with you. You are to bring into the ark two of all living creatures, male and female, to keep them alive with you. . . ."

Noah did everything just as God commanded him. (Genesis 6:5-22)

God looked upon the state of the world and saw that the spirit of Cain had prevailed, He saw that men had become full of wickedness, violence, and deceit; therefore, He decided to destroy all that He had created. But there was one man, Noah, who stood out among the wicked as someone worth saving, one man who refused to give in to his adversarial self, and as a result, found favor in the eyes of the Lord. In fact, this is what it means when the story says that Noah "walked with God"[250]—it means Noah successfully embodied the logos described in Genesis 1 and 2, that he embraced the attitude of Abel, and tried to make things better instead of worse, that he lived truthfully and courageously in the face of his vulnerabilities, and, unlike Adam, did not hide from God when he was called but instead sought what he knew to be right.

As a result of embracing the attitude of Abel and trying to make things better, Noah paid attention and could hear God calling him to build an ark, a call that he acknowledges and courageously accepts despite having no proof of an impending cataclysmic flood. And once Noah builds this ark and gets his family on board, God sends a flood that destroys the whole world, except for Noah and his family.

After studying the many flood myths that exist throughout the world, Mircea Eliade, a famous historian of religions, came to the conclusion that in mythology, the world is usually destroyed for one of two reasons: either things fall apart all by themselves (straight entropy), or they fall apart as a result of the sins of man.[251] Now remember, the word *sin* means *to miss the mark or target*, so the idea here is, if there are not enough people hitting the target or doing what they know to be right, then things will become so corrupt and unstable that, according to mythology, society will collapse and a flood of chaos will come rushing in and wash everything away.[252]

When hurricane Katrina caused New Orleans to flood in 2005, many people considered that event to be a natural disaster. But there is another way to think about it, especially if we want to understand what Mircea Eliade was talking about. The Dutch build their dikes strong enough to keep the ocean back because if they did not, Holland would be underwater. And when they were creating their dikes, the

Dutch estimated the worst possible oceanic storm that could occur in the next ten thousand years, and then built their dikes to withstand that storm.[253] Now, the Army Corp of Engineers built the levees in New Orleans strong enough to withstand the worst possible storm in the next one hundred years, *and they knew that would be insufficient.* Not only that, but New Orleans also has a reputation for corruption—it's often difficult to properly fund projects in New Orleans because the money intended for one project will be taken and used for something completely different, which means nothing really gets fixed.[254] And so, when a hurricane eventually hit New Orleans, the levees broke and the city flooded. Now, was this a natural disaster? In many ways it was, or at least that is one story we could tell. But we could also tell another story about the corruption of men and how the continual failure of people to hit the target caused a great flood that nearly wiped out an entire city.[255] And it is *this* version of the story that our ancestors were more interested in telling because it teaches a moral lesson about how we should behave in the future.

There will be times in our lives when we experience a flood, and it would be helpful if we knew how to build an ark and ride out the storm. This is exactly what the story of Noah teaches us. It tells us that Noah was a man who walked with God, that he was someone who tried to make things better instead of worse, that he chose to embody the attitude of Abel instead of the attitude of Cain, and as a result, he paid attention and could hear God calling him when it mattered most. The story of Noah tells us that the individuals who live in this manner—the individuals who do what they know to be right and listen to what they are being called to do—will not only save themselves and their families when the flood waters come, but they will also save the rest of humanity.

## Recap

- Sacrifice is mankind's hypothesis on how to minimize future suffering.
- The ritual act of sacrifice is an embodied representation of the idea of delayed gratification—it is the idea that giving up something we value in the present will result in future gain.

- The story of Cain and Abel is a foundational story of Western civilization. It is a story that says there are a twin pair of forces operating in the human psyche that can be conceptualized as brothers who are murderously opposed to one another.[256] And it is ultimately up to each individual to choose which personality he or she will manifest.
- The Bible says Noah was a man who walked with God, which means that he was always trying to make things better instead of worse—it means that Noah chose to embody the personality of Abel instead of the personality of Cain—and, unlike Adam, did not hide from God when he was called to do something.
- The story of Noah teaches us that if we choose the attitude of Abel—that is, if we aim at making things better and do what we know to be right—then we will be able to hear what God is calling us to do. And by obeying the call of God, we will not only have a chance to save ourselves and our families from destruction, but we will also have a chance to save all of mankind.

# CHAPTER FOURTEEN

---

# The Good News

EVERY CULTURE HAS A STORY and every story a hero. And whether we like it or not, the hero of our story—that is, the character who embodies the values upon which our civilization was built—is Jesus Christ. In the New Testament, there are four books that recount the story of Jesus—Matthew, Mark, Luke, and John—and these four books are typically referred to as "gospels," a word derived from a Greek word meaning "good news." Within these stories are the teachings of Jesus—the West's hypothesis on how to transcend our suffering and ultimately live lives full of meaning and purpose.

The story of Jesus begins with an angel visiting a young virgin girl named Mary and telling her that she will give birth to a son. This obviously comes as a shock to Mary, being a virgin and all, but because she is a servant of the Lord, she accepts what God has called her to do and prepares to have a child.[257]

As she awaits the arrival of her son, Mary and her soon-to-be husband Joseph travel to a town called Bethlehem in order to register for a census. Once they arrive, Mary gives birth to Jesus and lays him in a manger, as there was no more room left for them in the inn—a subtle, yet unmistakable reference to the hero's humble beginnings.[258]

According to the story, Jesus grows up in wisdom, stature, and favor with the Lord,[259] and before embarking on his ministry, decides to get baptized.[260] Now, we learn from the man who baptizes Jesus that the purpose of baptism is repentance.[261] Essentially, the ritual act of baptism is a symbolic representation of making a change in one's life. It is to say, "Here are all the ways that I have been missing the mark, and starting now, I will live differently." It is to acknowledge that we don't know everything there is to know, to embrace the role of the fool, and to decide to value and pursue redemptive knowledge above all things. Therefore, by choosing to become baptized, Jesus adopts an attitude of humility and makes the decision to seek truth above all things in his life. And as a result of this decision, a light shines down on Jesus from heaven and the voice of God is heard saying, "This is my Son, whom I love; with him I am well pleased."[262]

After Jesus makes the decision to humble himself and value the truth above all things, the story then says that he is "led by the Spirit into the desert to be tempted by the devil."[263]

## Tempted in the Desert

In Christian mythology, Satan is the eternal adversary. He is the personality who rejects truth in favor of the lie, the attitude that refuses to admit to error and therefore denies any need for repentance. He is the personification of evil itself, and the spirit who refuses to make the proper sacrifices out of spite.[264] Satan is that part of our psyche that does not want to make things better, that part that rationalizes and tempts us to do the things we know are wrong. And so not long after Jesus repents and chooses the direction of his life, he is led into the desert where he is tempted by the devil, the worst part of himself.

> Then Jesus was led by the Spirit into the desert to be tempted by the devil. After fasting forty days and forty nights, he was hungry. The tempter came to him and said, "If you are the Son of God, tell these stones to become bread."
>
> Jesus answered, "It is written: 'Man does not live on bread alone, but on every word that comes from the mouth of God.'" (Matthew 4:1–4)

Fasting is a religious discipline where one abstains from eating any food for an extended period of time; and when done alongside prayer and mediation, fasting can be used to strengthen one's spiritual life and connection to God. Now the Bible tells us that "God is love,"[265] and so when we read that Jesus is fasting in the desert, we are supposed to make the connection that he is devoting himself to God and therefore devoting himself to the spirit of love, truth, and making things better. But forty days without food is a long time, and the devil is patient. As soon as Jesus begins to acknowledge that he is hungry, Satan jumps in and tries to get him to break his fast, and therefore *his devotion to God*, by tempting him to turn some nearby stones into bread. Satan looks at a starving Jesus and says something like, "Come on, you have proven your point! You are starving! Why don't you turn these stones into bread and eat something?" Although tempted, Jesus knows in his heart that this would be wrong and responds by saying, "Man does not live on bread alone, but on every word that comes from the mouth of God."

The way Jesus responds to this first temptation indicates a couple of important things. First, Jesus says, "Man does not live on bread alone," implying that there is more to life than just staying alive—that there is actually another type of life worth striving for and placing above mere survival. And second, that this type of life can only be attained through "every word that comes from the mouth of God," meaning that it can only be attained through something like spiritual nourishment. And so when Jesus, in the face of his own starvation, is tempted to abandon his devotion to God, truth, and making things better, we find that he would rather risk his own life than jeopardize his soul.

> Christ responds to the first temptation by saying, "One does not live by bread alone, but by every word that proceeds from the mouth of God." What does this answer mean? It means that even under conditions of extreme privation, there are more important things than food. To put it another way: Bread is of little use to the man who has betrayed his soul, even if he is currently starving. Christ could clearly use his near-infinite power, as Satan indicates, to gain bread, now—to break his fast . . . But at what cost? And to what gain? Gluttony, in the midst of moral destitution? That's the poorest and most miserable of feasts. Christ aims, therefore, at something higher: at the description of a mode of Being that would finally and forever solve the problem of hunger. If we all chose instead of

expedience to dine on the Word of God? That would require each and every person to live, and produce, and sacrifice, and speak, and share in a manner that would permanently render the privation of hunger a thing of the past. And that's how the problem of hunger in the privations of the desert is most truly and finally addressed.[266]

And after Jesus successfully overcomes this first temptation, Satan wastes no time in trying again, only this time from a different angle.

Then the devil took him to the holy city and had him stand on the highest point of the temple. "If you are the Son of God," he said, "throw yourself down. For it is written:

"'He will command his angels concerning you, and they will lift you up in their hands, so that you will not strike your foot against a stone.'"

Jesus answered him, "It is also written: 'Do not put the Lord your God to the test.'" (Matthew 4:5–7)

For his second attempt, Satan takes Jesus to the top of a tall building and says, "How do you *really* know you are the son of God—don't you want proof? Throw yourself off this ledge, and if you are truly God's son, His angels will save you." Here we find Jesus, like all men, tempted to doubt who he is and what he has been called to do, tempted to demand proof that he is someone who can make things better before believing it is so. But in the midst of his doubt, Jesus stands his ground and chooses to have faith, chooses to turn away from Satan and put his trust in God by responding, "I will not demand God prove Himself to me; I know who I am and what I have been called to do." And with that, Satan, in a final act of desperation, drags Jesus to the top of a mountain to tempt him one last time.

Again, the devil took him to a very high mountain and showed him all the kingdoms of the world and their splendor. "All this I will give you," he said, "if you will bow down and worship me."

Jesus said to him, "Away from me, Satan! For it is written: 'Worship the Lord your God, and serve him only.'"

Then the devil left him, and angels came and attended him. (Matthew 4:8–11)

In a last ditch effort, Satan offers Jesus the world. He tells Jesus that he can have everything—all the wealth, status, and pleasure the world has to offer—all he has to do is place his own selfish desires above his commitment to God. But Jesus, having already made the decision to value love and truth above all things, rebukes Satan and commands him to leave, thus, dispensing with the final temptation.

These three temptations that Jesus encounters in the desert are perhaps the three most fundamental temptations that we all face in life: (1) to value survival over spiritual growth; (2) to doubt our importance and what we are being called to do, and (3) to place our selfish desires above what we know to be right. The writings produced by the twentieth-century concentration camps do an exceptional job of highlighting this very fact. Indeed, the conditions of camp life were extreme, but camp life is still life, and it was these extreme conditions that allowed the noise of everyday life to die down and the voice of the devil to be heard more clearly. In fact, camp life "is analogous to normal life in all its facets, but made starker, less ambiguous, clarified, laid bare."[267] And when we read about such a life, we can't help but ask ourselves how we would respond under such extreme conditions—how we would respond if we found ourselves starving in the desert, being tempted by the devil himself. Aleksandr Solzhenitsyn recounts his experience in the Soviet Union gulag:

> The overcrowding of the cells not only took the place of the tightly confined solitary "box" but also assumed the character of a first-class *torture* in itself . . . The jailers pushed so many prisoners into the cell that not every one had even a piece of floor; some were sitting on others' feet, and people walked on people and couldn't even move about at all. . . .
> In this "kennel" there was neither ventilation nor a window, and the prisoners' body heat and breathing raised the temperature to 40 or 45 degrees Centigrade—104 to 113 degrees Fahrenheit—and everyone sat there in undershorts with their winter clothing piled beneath them. Their naked

bodies were pressed against one another, and they got eczema from one another's sweat. They sat like that for *weeks at a time,* and were given neither fresh air nor water—except for gruel and tea in the morning.[268]

In cold lower than 60 degrees below zero [!], workdays were written off: in other words, on such days the records showed that the workers had not gone out to work; but they chased them out anyway, and whatever they squeezed out of them on those days was added to the other days, thereby raising the percentages. (And the servile Medical Section wrote off those who froze to death on such cold days on some other basis. And the ones who were left who could no longer walk and were straining every sinew to crawl along on all fours on the way back to camp, the convoy simply shot, so that they wouldn't escape before they could come back to get them).[269]

Concentration camp survivor, Viktor Frankl, adds:

Like nearly all the camp inmates I was suffering from edema. My legs were so swollen and the skin on them so tightly stretched that I could scarcely bend my knees. I had to leave my shoes unlaced in order to make them fit my swollen feet. There would not have been space for socks even if I had had any. So my partly bare feet were always wet and my shoes always full of snow. This, of course, caused frostbite and chilblains. Every single step became real torture. Clumps of ice formed on our shoes during our marches over snow covered fields....[270]

During the latter part of our imprisonment, the daily ration consisted of very watery soup given out once daily, and the usual small bread ration....

When the last layers of subcutaneous fat had vanished, and we looked like skeletons disguised with skin and rags, we could watch our bodies beginning to devour themselves. The organism digested its own protein, and the muscles disappeared....

The most ghastly moment of the twenty-four hours of camp life was the awakening, when, at a still nocturnal hour, the three shrill blows of a whistle tore us pitilessly from our exhausted sleep and from the longings in our dreams. We then began the tussle with our wet shoes, into which we could scarcely force our feet, which were sore and swollen with edema. And there were the usual moans and groans about petty troubles, such as the snapping of wires which replaced shoelaces. One morning I heard someone, whom I knew to be brave and dignified, cry like a child because he finally had to go to the snowy marching grounds in his bare feet, as his shoes were too shrunken for him to wear. In those ghastly minutes, I found a little bit of comfort; a small piece of bread which I drew out of my pocket and munched with absorbed delight.[271]

In the twentieth-century concentration camp, many people found that they had stumbled into the desert, that they had been thrown into a place that would test them, a place where they would be tempted and enticed towards the darkest of human emotions.

Bread is not issued in equal pieces, but thrown onto a pile—go grab! Knock down your neighbors, and tear it out of their hands! The quantity of bread issued is such that one or two people have to die for each that survives. The bread is hung up on a pine tree—go fell it. The bread is deposited in a coal mine—go down and mine it. Can you think about your own grief, about the past and the future, about humanity and God? Your mind is absorbed in vain calculations which for the present moment cut you off from the heavens—and tomorrow are worth nothing. You *hate* labor—it is your principal enemy. You hate your companions—rivals in life and death. You are reduced to a frazzle by intense *envy* and alarm lest somewhere behind your back others are right now dividing up that bread which could be yours, that somewhere on the other side of the wall a tiny potato is being ladled out of the pot which could have ended up in your bowl.[272]

For many, when placed in such extreme conditions and forced to face their inner darkness, the thirst for survival takes over, and the luxury of living by one's conscience becomes a thing of the past.

Then there begins the period of transit prisons. Interspersed with our thoughts about our future camp, we now love to recall our past: How well we used to live! (Even if we lived badly.) But how many unused opportunities there were! How many flowers we left uncrumpled! . . . When will we now make up for it? If I only manage to survive—oh, how differently, how wisely, I am going to live! The day of our future *release*? It shines like a rising sun!

And the conclusion is: Survive to reach it! Survive! At any price!

This is simply a turn of phrase, a sort of habit of speech: "at any price."

But then the words swell up with their full meaning, and an awesome vow takes shape: to survive *at any price.*

And whoever takes that vow, whoever does not blink before its crimson burst—allows his own misfortune to overshadow both the entire common misfortune and the whole world.

This is the great fork of camp life. From this point the roads go to the right and to the left. One of them will rise, and the other will descend. If you go to the right—you lose your life, and if you go to the left—you lose your conscience. . . .

Let us admit the truth: At that great fork in the camp road, at the great divider of souls, it was not the majority of prisoners that turned to the right.[273]

And once conscience is abandoned and a vow is taken to survive at any price, things become tragically simple, and the ends begin to justify the means—

Let us take the case of a transport which was officially announced to transfer a certain number of prisoners to another camp; but it was a fairly safe guess that its final destination would be the gas chambers. A selection of sick or feeble prisoners incapable of work would be sent to one of the big central camps which were fitted with gas chambers and crematoriums. The selection process was the signal for a free fight among all the prisoners, or a group against group. All that mattered was that one's own name and that of one's friend were crossed off the list of victims, though everyone knew that for each man saved another victim had to be found. . . .

There was neither time nor desire to consider moral or ethical issues. Every man was controlled by one thought only: to keep himself alive for the family waiting for him at home, and to save his friends. With no hesitation, therefore, he would arrange for another prisoner, another "number," to take his place in the transport.[274]

—for when survival is king, no impulse is off-limits, and no behavior is too far. Frankl continues:

The process of selecting Capos was a negative one; only the most brutal of the prisoners were chosen for this job (although there were some happy exceptions). But apart from the selection of Capos which was undertaken by the SS, there was a sort of self-selecting process going on the whole time among all of the prisoners.

On the average, only those prisoners could keep alive who, after years of trekking from camp to camp, had lost all scruples in their fight for existence; they were prepared to use every means, honest and otherwise, even brutal force, theft, and betrayal of their friends, in order to save themselves. . . .[275]

Many of the Capos fared better in the camp than they had in their entire lives. Often they were harder on the prisoners than were the guards, and beat them more cruelly than the SS men did.[276]

Likewise, Solzhenitsyn:

You—had fallen. You—were punished. You—had been uprooted from life—but you want to avoid the very bottom of the pile? You want to hover over someone else, rifle in hand? Over your brother? Here! Take it! And if he runs—shoot him! We will even call you *comrade*. And we will give you a Red Army man's ration.

And . . . he grows proud. And . . . he tightens his grip on
his gun stock. And . . . he shoots. And . . . he is even more
severe than the free guards. (How is one to understand this:
Was it really a purblind faith in social initiative? Or was it just
an icy, contemptuous calculation based on the lowest human
feelings?)[277]

But not everyone who was tempted chose the road to the left; not
everyone, when faced with likelihood of their death, made this vow
of surviving at any price . . . *for man cannot live on bread alone.*

Here we have been breaking our backs for years at All-Union
hard labor. Here in slow annual spirals we have been climbing
up to an understanding of life—and from this height it can
all be seen so clearly: It is not the result that counts! It is not
the result—but *the spirit!* Not *what*—but *how.* Not what has
been attained—but at what price. . . .[278]

And how can one explain that certain unstable people found
faith right there in the camp, that they were strengthened by
it, and that they survived uncorrupted?

And many more, scattered about and unnoticed, came
to their allotted turning point and made no mistake in their
choice. Those who managed to see that things were not only
bad for them, but even worse, even harder, for their neighbors.

And all those who, under the threat of penalty zone and a
new term of imprisonment, refused to become stoolies?

How, in general, can one explain Grigory Ivanovich Grigoryev, a soil scientist? A scientist who volunteered for the People's
Volunteer Corps in 1941—and the rest of the story is a familiar
one. Taken prisoner near Vyazma, he spent his whole captivity
in a German camp. And the subsequent story is also familiar.
When he returned [to Russia], he was arrested by us and given
a tenner. I came to know him in winter, engaged in general
work in Ekibastuz. His forthrightness gleamed from his big
quiet eyes, some sort of unwavering forthrightness. This man
was never able to bow in spirit. And he didn't bow in camp,
either, even though he worked only two of his ten years in

his own field of specialization, and didn't receive food parcels from home for nearly the whole term. He was subjected on all sides to the camp philosophy, to the camp corruption of soul, but he was incapable of adopting it. In the Kemerovo camps (Antibess) the security chief kept trying to recruit him as a stoolie. Grigoryev replied to him quite honestly and candidly: "I find it quite repulsive to talk to you. You will find many willing without me." "You bastard, you'll crawl on all fours." "I would be better off hanging myself from the first branch." And so he was sent off to a penalty situation. He stood it for about half a year. And he made *mistakes* which were even more unforgivable: When he was sent on an agricultural work party, he refused (as a soil scientist) to accept the post of brigadier offered him. He hoed and scythed with enthusiasm. And even more stupidly: in Ekibastuz at the stone quarry he refused to be a work checker—only because he would have had to pad the work sheets for the sloggers, for which, later on, when they caught up with it, the eternally drunk free foreman would have to pay the penalty (but would he?). And so he went to break rocks! His honesty was so monstrously unnatural that when he went out to process potatoes with the vegetable storeroom brigade, he did not steal any, though everyone else did. When he was in a good post, in the privileged repair-shop brigade at the pumping-station equipment, he left simply because he refused to wash the socks of the free bachelor construction supervisor, Treivish. (His fellow brigade members tried to persuade him: Come on now, isn't it all the same, the kind of work you do? But no, it turned out it was not all the same to him!) How many times did he select the worst and hardest lot, just so as not to have to offend against his conscience—and he didn't, not in the least, and I am a witness. And even more: because of the astounding influence on his body of his bright and spotless human spirit (though no one today believes in any such influence, no one understands it) the organism of Grigory Ivanovich, who was no longer young (close to fifty), grew stronger in camp; his earlier rheumatism of the joints disappeared completely, and he became particularly healthy after the typhus from which he recovered: in winter, he went out in cotton sacks, making holes in them for his head and his arms—and he did not catch cold![279]

You see, although many became corrupted in camp, it appears this corruption had nothing to do with the camp conditions themselves, as horrible as they were. The extreme conditions of camp life only served to shine a light on the attitudes and decisions people had already made prior to being arrested—decisions to choose security over conscience, to value survival over soul.[280]

Those people became corrupted in camp who had already been corrupted out in freedom or who were ready for it. Because people are corrupted in freedom too, sometimes even more effectively than in camp.

The convoy officer who ordered that Moiseyevaite be tied to a post in order to be mocked—had he not been corrupted more profoundly than the camp inmates who spat on her?

And for that matter did every one of the brigade member spit on her? Perhaps only two from each brigade did. In fact, that is probably what happened.

Tatyana Falike writes: "Observation of people convinced me that no man could become a scoundrel in camp if he had not been one before."

If a person went swiftly bad in camp, what it might mean was that he had not just gone bad, but that that inner foulness which had not previously been needed had disclosed itself.

Voichenko has his opinion: "In camp, existence did not determine consciousness, but just the opposite: consciousness and steadfast faith in the human essence decided whether you became an animal or remained a human being."

A drastic, sweeping declaration! . . . But he was not the only one who thought so. The artist Ivashev-Musatov passionately argued exactly the same thing.[281]

These are the same decisions, the same temptations, that confront us in each moment of every day. Will we try to make things better, or will we try to make things worse? Will we place our selfish desires above what we know to be right, or will we turn away from temptation and value God above all things? Frankl states:

> It is apparent that the mere knowledge that a man was either a camp guard or a prisoner tells us almost nothing. Human kindness can be found in all groups, even those which as a whole it would be easy to condemn. The boundaries between groups overlapped and we must not try to simplify matters by saying that these men were angels and those were devils. . . . I remember how one day a foreman secretly gave me a piece of bread which I knew he must have saved from his breakfast ration. It was far more than the small piece of bread which moved me to tears at that time. It was the human "something" which this man also gave to me—the word and look which accompanied the gift.
>
> From all this we may learn that there are two races of men in this world, but only these two—the "race" of the decent man and the "race" of the indecent man. Both are found everywhere; they penetrate into all groups of society. No group consists entirely of decent or indecent people. In this sense, no group is of "pure race"—and therefore one occasionally found a decent fellow among the camp guards.[282]

An idea that Solzhenitsyn echoes:

> It was granted me to carry away from my prison years on my bent back, which nearly broke beneath its load, this essential experience: *how* a human being becomes evil and *how* good. In the intoxication of youthful successes I had felt myself to be infallible, and I was therefore cruel. In the surfeit of power I was a murderer, and an oppressor. In my most evil moments I was convinced that I was doing good, and I was well supplied with systematic arguments. And it was only when I lay there on rotting prison straw that I sensed within myself the first stirrings of good. Gradually it was disclosed to me that the line separating good and evil passes not through states, nor

between classes, nor between political parties either—but right
through every human heart—and through all human hearts.[283]

And finally, Frankl again:

We who lived in concentration camps can remember the men
who walked through the huts comforting others, giving away
their last piece of bread. They may have been few in number,
but they offer sufficient proof that everything can be taken
from a man but one thing: the last of the human freedoms—
to choose one's attitude in any given set of circumstances, to
choose one's own way.

And there were always choices to make. Every day, every
hour, offered the opportunity to make a decision, a decision
which determined whether you would or would not submit
to those powers which threatened to rob you of your very self,
your inner freedom; which determined whether or not you
would become the plaything of circumstance, renouncing
freedom and dignity to become moulded into the form of
the typical inmate.

Seen from this point of view, the mental reactions of
the inmates of a concentration camp must seem more to us
than the mere expression of certain physical and sociological
conditions. Even though conditions such as lack of sleep,
insufficient food and various mental stresses may suggest
that the inmates were bound to react in certain ways, in the
final analysis it becomes clear that the sort of person the
prisoner became was the result of an inner decision, and not
the result of camp influences alone. Fundamentally, therefore,
any man can, even under such circumstances, decide what
shall become of him—mentally and spiritually... it is this
spiritual freedom—which cannot be taken away—that makes
life meaningful and purposeful.[284]

Before heading out into the world, Jesus humbled himself through
baptism and *made the decision* to value God—love, truth, and making things better—above all things. Therefore, when he eventually

found himself in the desert being tempted by the devil, he had the strength necessary to overcome these temptations and stay true to his devotion to God.

## The Kingdom of God

After making the decision to serve God above all things, Jesus then sets out to accomplish what he has been called to do—namely, travel the land and teach people about *the kingdom of God.* But what is this mysterious kingdom? For starters, we learn that it is not a physical place, but rather, a place that we experience, a place that exists within the world of meaning as opposed to the world of objects:

> Once, having been asked by the Pharisees when the kingdom of God would come, Jesus replied, "The Kingdom of God does not come with your careful observation, nor will people say, 'Here it is,' or 'There it is,' because the kingdom of God is within you." (Luke 17:20–21)

It has also been said that by entering into the kingdom of God we will obtain something called *eternal life*—that is, a type of life not defined by its duration but rather by its quality; a type of life that cannot be taken away or destroyed and that fills us with the meaning and purpose necessary to face the tragedy of existence and prevail.

But how can such a place be reached? Well, we can infer through Jesus' teachings that this kingdom can only be discovered by those who are willing to place their conscience above all things, regardless of the consequences—

> Blessed are those who are persecuted because of righteousness, for theirs is the kingdom of heaven. (Matthew 5:10)

*—it is a place that can only be discovered by those who choose to identify with the hero,* by those who value and pursue redemptive knowledge above all things, by those who strive to become true individuals, and therefore are willing to stand outside of the group unaccepted, seen as

different, weak, and inferior to those who belong to the crowd. Such is why it is said that "only the unredeemed—the outcast, the sick, the blind, and the lame—can be 'saved.'"[285]

At its very core, it could be said that the kingdom of God is a place that can only be discovered by those who value God above all things; by those who place the truth over their survival, and their spiritual growth above earthly gain.

> Now a man came up to Jesus and asked, "Teacher, what good thing must I do to get eternal life?"
>
> "Why do you ask me about what is good?" Jesus replied. "There is only One who is good. If you want to enter life, obey the commandments."
>
> "Which ones?" the man inquired.
>
> Jesus replied, "'Do not murder, do not commit adultery, do not steal, do not give false testimony, honor your father and mother, and love your neighbor as yourself.'"
>
> "All of these I have kept," the young man said. "What do I still lack?"
>
> Jesus answered, "If you want to be perfect, go, sell your possessions and give to the poor, and you will have treasure in heaven. Then come, follow me."
>
> When the young man heard this, he went away sad, because he had great wealth.
>
> Then Jesus said to his disciples, "I tell you the truth, it is hard for a rich man to enter the kingdom of heaven. Again, I tell you, it is easier for a camel to go through the eye of a needle than for a rich man to enter the kingdom of God." (Matthew 19:16–24)

It's not that worldly pleasures and earthly gain are bad things in and of themselves, but instead it is our *attachment* to these things—choosing to value them above God, truth, and what we know to be right—that will stop us from reaching this eternal kingdom.

Jesus replied: "A certain man was preparing a great banquet and invited many guests. At the time of the banquet he sent his servant to tell those who had been invited, 'Come, for everything is now ready.'

But they all alike began to make excuses. The first said, 'I have just bought a field, and I must go and see it. Please excuse me.'

Another said, 'I have just bought five yoke of oxen, and I'm on my way to try them out. Please excuse me.'

Still another said, 'I just got married, so I can't come.'

The servant came back and reported this to his master. Then the owner of the house became angry and ordered his servant, 'Go out quickly into the streets and alleys of the town and bring in the poor, the crippled, the blind and the lame.'

'Sir,' the servant said, 'what you ordered has been done, but there is still room.'

Then the master told his servant, 'Go out to the roads and country lanes and make them come in, so that my house will be full. I tell you, not one of those men who were invited will get a taste of my banquet.'" (Luke 14:16–24)

This is because there will be times in our lives when we are forced to make tough decisions, and when those times come, if we have chosen to value anything above God, then we will be unwilling to sacrifice those things for what we know to be right.

"Do not store up for yourselves treasure on earth, where moth and rust destroy, and where thieves break in and steal. But store up for yourselves treasures in heaven, where moth and rust do not destroy, and where thieves do not break in and steal. For where your treasure is, there your heart will be also. . . .

No one can serve two masters. Either he will hate the one and love the other, or he will be devoted to the one and despise the other. You cannot serve both God and money." (Matthew 6:19–24)

The kingdom of God is a place that can only be discovered by those who put God first; by those who listen to their conscience and obey what God is calling them to do.

188 The World of Meaning

There is a sport in Harry Potter called *quidditch*, which is more or less basketball on brooms. While both teams are playing broom-basketball, there is one player from each team called a *seeker* who is playing an entirely different game. The job of the seeker is to find and catch something called the *golden snitch*—a very small ball that flies around incredibly fast—and as soon as one of the seekers catches this golden snitch, the quidditch game is over and their team wins. Like seekers, when we value God above all things, we are choosing to play a different game than everyone else. Instead of following the crowd and playing the safety, wealth, and survival game, we are choosing to play the soul, truth, and conscience game—a higher and more important game to be playing. And once we choose to play this game, certain meanings will begin to shine forth to us from the unknown; they will grab our attention and call us forward like a golden snitch. And like seekers chasing that snitch, if we want to win the game and enter into the kingdom of God, it is our job to listen to our conscience and follow these meanings wherever they may lead.

We all have something unique calling to us, our own personal snitch to chase—in its essence, this is what it means to be called on by God. The biblical call of God is that thing deep in our gut that we know we must do. It is that which calls to us from the unknown and is what will ultimately lead us to our life's purpose.

> As Jesus was saying these things, a woman in the crowd called out, "Blessed is the mother who gave you birth and nursed you."
> He replied, "Blessed rather are those who hear the word of God and obey it." (Luke 11:27–28)

Now keep in mind, the call of God has nothing to do with our own selfish desires—although that doesn't mean it can't ever coincide with the things we enjoy doing—but rather, it revolves around doing the things that we know we *must* do, doing the things that make us feel stronger, and avoiding the things that make us feel weak. Thus, to obey the call of God is ultimately to do what we know to be right, while avoiding what we know to be wrong. And if we listen to what we are being called to do and choose to follow that call faithfully, then Jesus tells us we will enter into the kingdom of God and receive everlasting life.

> These are the secret sayings which the living Jesus spoke and which Didymos Judas Thomas wrote down.
> And he said, "Whoever finds the interpretation of these sayings will not experience death."
> Jesus said, "Let him who seeks continue seeking until he finds. When he becomes troubled, he will be astonished, and he will rule over all."
> Jesus said, "If those who lead you say to you, 'See, the kingdom is in the sky,' then the birds of the sky will precede you. If they say to you, 'It is in the sea,' then the fish will precede you. Rather, the kingdom is inside of you, and it is outside of you. When you come to know yourselves, then you will become known, and you will realize that it is you who are the sons of the living father. But if you will not know yourselves, you dwell in poverty and it is you who are that poverty."
> Jesus said, "The man old in days will not hesitate to ask a small child seven days old about the place of life, and he will live. For many who are first will become last, and they will become one and the same."
> Jesus said, "Recognize what is in your sight, and that which is hidden from you will become plain to you. For there is nothing hidden which will not become manifest."
> His disciples questioned him and said to him, "Do you want us to fast? How shall we pray? Shall we give alms? What diet shall we observe?"
> Jesus said, "Do not tell lies, and do not do what you hate, for all things are plain in the sight of heaven. For nothing hidden will not become manifest, and nothing covered will remain without being uncovered."[286]

Before we can enter the kingdom of God, we first have to make the decision to value God—love, truth, and making things better—above all things. And once we have made that decision, Jesus then indicates the final step to entering this kingdom is to have faith in the outcome, an idea we learn more about in one of his most famous sermons, the *Sermon on the Mount*:

> "Therefore I tell you, do not worry about your life, what you will eat or drink; or about your body, what you will wear. Is not life more important than food, and the body more important than clothes? Look at the birds of the air; they do not sow or reap or store away in barns, and yet your heavenly Father feeds them. Are you not much more valuable than they? Who of you by worrying can add a single hour to his life?
>
> And why do you worry about clothes? See how the lilies of the field grow. They do not labor or spin. Yet I tell you that not even Solomon in all his splendor was dressed like one of these. If that is how God clothes the grass of the field, which is here today and tomorrow is thrown into the fire, will he not much more clothe you, O you of little faith? So do not worry, saying, 'What shall we eat?' or 'What shall we drink?' or 'What shall we wear?' For the pagans run after all these things, and your heavenly Father knows that you need them. But seek first his kingdom and his righteousness, and all these things will be given to you as well. Therefore do not worry about tomorrow, for tomorrow will worry about itself. Each day has enough trouble of its own. (Matthew 6:25–34)

This brief excerpt from Jesus' sermon is often misinterpreted as advocating for people to live like hippies and follow their bliss—that if people would just do what made them happy and not worry about anything else, then everything would turn out just fine. But that isn't what this verse means. Not even a little bit. Jesus is not saying "hakuna matata," but rather, he is saying that before we do anything, *we must first seek the kingdom of God*—which means that we must decide to value God, truth, and making things better above all things—*and then* not worry about tomorrow. This is a wildly different interpretation than what we are typically led to believe. Jesus is not saying, "Don't worry, be happy," he is saying we first have to aim properly and do what we know to be right, and once that is done, then we can live in the moment and have faith in the outcome.

After we choose to value God above all things, Jesus implies that *having faith* is the final step to reaching the kingdom of God, an idea that is beautifully illustrated throughout the gospels. Throughout the gospels, while Jesus teaches his followers about the kingdom of God, he also performs many miracles. And as he performs these miracles, he almost always attributes their occurrence, not to his own divine power, but rather to an individual's faith in him—that is, an individual's faith in the embodied logos; an individual's faith in the idea that acting out the spirit of "truth motivated by love" will result in good things.

When a blind man asks Jesus to restore his sight, Jesus responds with, "Go . . . your faith has healed you."[287] When a sick woman secretly touches Jesus' cloak believing it would heal her, Jesus says, "Daughter, your faith has healed you. Go in peace and be freed from your suffering."[288] When a centurion tells Jesus his servant back home is paralyzed, but that he believes Jesus could heal his servant by merely saying the word, a shocked Jesus turns to his followers and says, "I tell you the truth, I have not found anyone in Israel with such great faith."[289] He then says to the centurion, "Go! It will be done just as you believed it would."[290]

Conversely, any time a miracle could not be performed, Jesus attributes the failure to a lack of faith. When Jesus' disciples ask him why they could not heal a demon-possessed man, Jesus replies, "Because you have so little faith. I tell you the truth, if you have faith as small as a mustard seed, you can say to this mountain, 'Move from here to there' and it will move. Nothing will be impossible for you."[291] At one point in the gospel of Matthew, Jesus walks on water so that he can join his disciples out on a lake—a dramatic representation of how the embodied logos will allow us to rise above the chaos in our lives. And when Peter, one of Jesus' disciples, sees Jesus coming towards them, he decides to leave the boat and meet Jesus halfway on the water. But not long after Peter leaves the boat, he becomes afraid and begins to sink into the watery chaos that surrounds him. Acting swiftly, Jesus reaches out his hand and catches Peter, saying, "You of little faith . . . why did you doubt?"[292] And lastly, when Jesus visits his hometown, no one believed his teachings, and as a result, he "could not do any miracles" and was "amazed at their lack of faith."[293]

Like Jesus in the desert, after we make the decision to value God above all things, we must then choose to have faith. And according to the gospels, if this is done properly, then it is the strength of our faith that will determine whether or not we experience miracles in our lives.

> Now faith is being sure of what we hope for and certain of what we do not see. This is what the ancients were commended for. . . .
>
> By faith Noah, when warned about things not yet seen, in holy fear built an ark to save his family. By his faith he condemned the world and became heir of the righteousness that comes by faith.
>
> By faith Abraham, when called to go to a place he would later receive as his inheritance, obeyed and went, even though he did not know where he was going. By faith he made his home in the promised land like a stranger in a foreign country . . .
>
> And what more shall I say? I do not have to tell you about Gideon, Barak, Samson, Jephthah, David, Samuel and the prophets, who through faith conquered kingdoms, administered justice, and gained what was promised; who shut the mouths of lions, quenched the fury of the flames, and escaped the edge of the sword; whose weakness was turned to strength; and who became powerful in battle and routed foreign armies. (Hebrews 11:1–9, 32–34)

According to the teachings of Jesus, placing God above all things, obeying what we are being called to do, and having faith in the outcome are the three most important steps for reaching the kingdom of God. Now what's interesting about this is, these three steps also seem to be the backbone of what is famously—or infamously, depending on whom you talk to—referred to as the *law of attraction*, a theory that essentially claims whatever we choose to concentrate on will end up manifesting in our lives. One of the most popular books on the law of attraction, *The Secret*, breaks this law down into three simple steps: ask, believe, and receive.

The first step of the law of attraction is about identifying a direction. Practitioners of the law of attraction typically center their ask around worldly pleasures and earthly gain, but if we adhere to the teachings of Jesus, we would approach this first step differently. That is, once we choose to value God above all things, we are then supposed to *ask* what it is we are being called to do, pay attention, and allow an answer to be revealed to us.

The second step of the law of attraction is to *believe*—this step is about having faith in what we are being called to do, despite having doubts. Having faith does not mean we should deceive ourselves about reality, as some would have us think, but rather, it is to fully acknowledge how we are experiencing the world, and then to trust that no matter the obstacle, we will overcome and accomplish what we have set out to do. Anyone who has ever accomplished anything worthwhile in their lives will say that they did not know how they were going to do it, they just knew deep down it was going to happen. Living by faith is not stupid, nor is it weak. Quite the contrary. Living by faith is a choice, and it is the ultimate expression of mental toughness.

> "I tell you the truth, if anyone says to this mountain, 'Go throw yourself into the sea,' and does not doubt in his heart but believes that what he says will happen, it will be done for him. Therefore I tell you, *whatever you ask for in prayer, believe that you have received it, and it will be yours.*" (Mark 11:22–24; italics added)

And lastly, the third and final step of the law of attraction is to *receive*, a step that requires action. To receive means to respond to the meanings we experience truthfully, to follow our snitch and to obey the call of God. And if we do this properly, the law of attraction claims that miracles will manifest in our lives as a result.

Believing in the law of attraction is not the same thing as believing in magic—it is to recognize that how we live in the world ultimately determines how life unfolds for us. Between the 1300s and the 1700s the study of alchemy became increasingly popular—a form of science which attempted to turn base metals into gold. And while it is easy to scoff at the idea of alchemy, we forget that ideas have to start somewhere; and just as astrology paved the way for astronomy, alchemy eventually transformed into what is now known as modern-day chemistry. Likewise, I think it is entirely possible that the law of attraction is still in its beginning stages of development and is a precursor to something very real and profound; a precursor to something mankind has yet to fully understand, although vital to the development of our species.

> "So I say to you: Ask and it will be given to you; seek and you will find; knock and the door will be opened to you. For everyone who asks receives; he who seeks finds; and to him who knocks, the door will be opened." (Luke 11:9)

And it is these three steps—choosing to value God above all things, having faith in what we are being called to do, and then acting on that faith—that, according to the gospels, will allow us to enter into the kingdom of God and experience eternal life.

## The Ultimate Sacrifice

As Jesus continued to travel the land and teach about the kingdom of God, his following grew so big that he eventually attracted the attention of the Jewish traditionalists and teachers of the law. Now Jesus' interpretation of the law was truly revolutionary for its time; his teachings not only challenged the status quo, but in doing so, also challenged the traditionalists themselves by implicitly questioning whether these leaders really deserved their lofty positions in society. Therefore, because these leaders felt threatened by Jesus, they set out to trap him in his words.

> Then the Pharisees went out and laid plans to trap him in his words. They sent their disciples to him along with the Herodians. "Teacher," they said, "we know you are a man of integrity and that you teach the way of God in accordance with the truth. You aren't swayed by men, because you pay no attention to who they are. Tell us then, what is your opinion? Is it right to pay taxes to Caesar or not?"
> But Jesus, knowing their evil intent, said, "You hypocrites, why are you trying to trap me? Show me the coin used for paying the tax." They brought him a denarius, and he asked them, "Whose portrait is this? And whose inscription?"

"Caesar's," they replied.

Then he said to them, "Give to Caesar what is Caesar's, and to God what is God's."

When they heard this, they were amazed. So they left him and went away. (Matthew 22:15–22)

In their first attempt to corner Jesus, we find that the Pharisees—the traditionalists who believe in a strict observance of the Jewish law—and the Herodians—a nonreligious political party who support the reign of Herod—have joined forces and ask Jesus if it is lawful to pay taxes to Caesar. For all intents and purposes, this is a lose-lose situation for Jesus, and he knows it. If he answers, "Yes," the Pharisees will convince the crowd he is a traitor to the Jewish people; but if he answers, "No," the Herodians will charge him with treason against Rome. And just as it was beginning to look like Jesus had met his match, he does something that no one expects; he answers their question while simultaneously avoiding their trap by saying something like, "The material world has no hold over the spiritual world. If Caesar demands his material payment, give it him! After all, his face *is* on the coin, is it not? So give to Caesar what is his, and give to God your spiritual life—your commitment to soul, conscience, and truth above all things." And after such a devastatingly brilliant answer, the Pharisees and Herodians were amazed by his wisdom, and left him, speechless.

One of them, an expert in the law, tested him with this question: Teacher, which is the greatest commandment in the Law?"

Jesus replied: "'Love the Lord your God with all your heart and with all your soul and with all your mind.' This is the first and the greatest commandment. And the second is like it: 'Love your neighbor as yourself.' All the Law and the Prophets hang on these two commandments." (Matthew 22:35–40)

At this point in the story, everyone begins taking shots at Jesus hoping that they can be the one to trip him up. And after Jesus successfully navigates each skillfully placed trap, we read that the Pharisees then send one of their best, an expert in the law, to bait Jesus into saying something heretical. Wasting no time, this expert approaches Jesus and innocently asks him to rank the Mosaic commandments in the order of their importance. But once again, Jesus completely sidesteps this trap by extracting out the essence of the law—*love God with all of your heart, and love your neighbor as yourself*—and says that this essence is more important than the actual laws themselves, for every commandment was ultimately created to serve this essence in the first place[294]—an idea that Jesus attempts to drive home many times throughout the gospels:

> One Sabbath Jesus was going through the grainfields, and his disciples began to pick some heads of grain, rub them in their hands and eat the kernels. Some of the Pharisees asked, "Why are you doing what is unlawful on the Sabbath?"
>
> Jesus answered them, "Have you never read what David did when he and his companions were hungry? He entered the house of God, and taking the consecrated bread, he ate what is lawful only for priests to eat. And he also gave some to his companions." Then Jesus said to them, "The Son of Man is Lord on the Sabbath."
>
> On another Sabbath he went into the synagogue and was teaching, and a man was there whose right hand was shriveled. The Pharisees and the teachers of the law were looking for a reason to accuse Jesus, so they watched him closely to see if he would heal on the Sabbath. But Jesus knew what they were thinking and said to the man with the shriveled hand, "Get up and stand in front of everyone." So he got up and stood there.
>
> Then Jesus said to them, "I ask you, which is lawful on the Sabbath: to do good or to do evil, to save life or to destroy it?"
>
> He looked around at them all, and then said to the man, "Stretch out your hand." He did so, and his hand was completely restored. (Luke 6:1–10)

Dr. Peterson comments further on the passage above in his book *Beyond Order*:

> An ancient document known as the Codex Bezea, a non-canonical variant of part of the New Testament, offers an

interpolation just after the section of the Gospel of Luke presented above, shedding profound light on the same issue. It offers deeper insight into the complex paradoxical relationship between respect for the rules and creative moral action that is necessary and desirable, despite manifesting itself in apparent opposition to those rules. It contains an account of Christ addressing someone who, like Him, has broken a sacred rule: "On that same day, observing one working on the Sabbath, [Jesus] said to him O Man, if indeed thou knowest what thou doest, thou art blest; but if thou knowest not, thou art accursed, and a transgressor of the Law."

What does this statement mean? . . . If you understand the rules—their necessity, their sacredness, the chaos they keep at bay, how they unite the communities that follow them, the price paid for their establishment, and the danger of breaking them—but you are willing to fully shoulder the responsibility of making an exception, because you see that as serving a higher good (and if you are a person with sufficient character to manage that distinction), then you have served the spirit, rather than the mere law, and that is an elevated moral act. But if you refuse to realize the importance of the rules you are violating and act out of self-centered convenience, then you are appropriately and inevitably damned.[295]

In the New Testament, the traditionalists and teachers of the law represent the stagnant element of tradition—the part of tradition that was once wise, but over time has grown old, blind, and set in its ways; they are the servants of dogma who have become too rigid in their thinking, too attached to the rules to understand their purpose and, therefore, have placed those rules, as well as the status those rules provide them, above even God Himself.

Then Jesus said to the crowds and to his disciples:
"The teachers of the law and the Pharisees sit in Moses' seat. So you must obey them and do everything they tell you. But do not do what they do, for they do not practice what they preach. They tie up heavy loads and put them on men's

shoulders, but they themselves are not willing to lift a finger
to move them.

"Everything they do is done for men to see: They make their
phylacteries wide and the tassels on their garments long; they
love the place of honor at banquets and the most important
seats in the synagogues; they love to be greeted in the market-
places and to have men call them 'Rabbi.'" (Matthew 23:1–7)

They refuse to repent, refuse to be baptized, refuse to acknowledge
that they don't know everything there is to know and, therefore, they
reject what God is calling them to do.[296] Collectively, they represent
the Tyrannical Father, who out of blind allegiance to order, suffocates
his own sons.

"Woe to you, teachers of the law and Pharisees, you hypocrites!
You shut the kingdom of heaven in men's faces. You yourselves
do not enter, nor will you let those enter who are trying to."
(Matthew 23:13)

And Jesus is the hero who chooses to place spirit over dogma, a
master of the rules who has learned when it is necessary to break those
selfsame rules in service of a higher good. Jesus is the individual who
strives to make things better, regardless of the cost; the one who is willing
to descend into the belly of the beast in order to rescue his father; and
he who travels to the underworld in order to give blind tradition sight.

"Do not think that I have come to abolish the Law or the
Prophets; I have not come to abolish them but to fulfill them.
. . . For I tell you that unless your righteousness surpasses that
of the Pharisees and the teachers of the law, you will certainly
not enter the kingdom of heaven. . . ."
Then some Pharisees and teachers of the law came to Jesus
from Jerusalem and asked, "Why do your disciples break the tradition of the elders? They don't wash their hands before they eat!"
Jesus replied, "And why do you break the command of God
for the sake of your tradition? . . . You hypocrites! Isaiah was
right when he prophesied about you:

"'These people honor me with their lips,
    but their hearts are far from me.
They worship me in vain;
    their teachings are but rules taught by men.'"

Jesus called the crowd to him and said, "Listen and understand. What goes into a man's mouth does not make him 'unclean,' but what comes out of his mouth, that is what makes him unclean.'"

Then the disciples came to him and asked, "Do you know that the Pharisees were offended when they heard this?"

He replied, "Every plant that my heavenly Father has not planted will be pulled up by the roots. Leave them; they are blind guides. If a blind man leads a blind man, both will fall into a pit. (Matthew 5:17,20; Matthew 15:1–14)

And as Jesus continues to outmaneuver the Pharisees and teachers of the law, they become increasingly impatient, and begin looking for ways to get rid of him once and for all. Now one of Jesus' closest disciples, Judas, was a greedy man—he was a man who had secretly made the decision to value material gain above all things[297]—and therefore, agreed to hand Jesus over to the Pharisees in exchange for thirty pieces of silver.[298] And as Jesus waits to be arrested by the Pharisees—for he knew that he had been betrayed by Judas—we find that he begins to struggle with what he knows God is calling him to do:

Then Jesus went with his disciples to a placed called Gethsemane, and he said to them, "Sit here while I go over there and pray." He took Peter and the two sons of Zebedee along with him, and he began to be sorrowful and troubled. Then he said to them, "My soul is overwhelmed with sorrow to the point of death. Stay here and keep watch with me."

Going a little farther, he fell with his face to the ground and prayed, "My Father, if it is possible, may this cup be taken from me. Yet not as I will, but as you will." (Matthew 26:36–39)

Like Adam, Jesus is afraid and wants to hide when he hears God calling. In fact, the gospel of Luke even says that Jesus is so overwhelmed with fear that he actually begins to sweat blood![299] But instead of hiding, Jesus takes a deep breath and prays. He consults his conscience. He looks to the sky and sincerely asks, "Is there another way?"

> Then he returned to his disciples and found them sleeping. "Could you men not keep watch with me for one hour?" he asked Peter. "Watch and pray so that you will not fall into temptation. The spirit is willing, but the body is weak."
> He went away a second time and prayed, "My Father, if it is not possible for this cup to be taken away unless I drink it, may your will be done." (Matthew 26:40–42)

Here we read that when Jesus returns and finds his disciples sleeping, he says, "the spirit is willing, but the body is weak," an acknowledgment that although we desperately want to live in truth, there will be times in life when that is easier said than done. He then looks at Peter and tells him that if he wants to do right, then he must pay attention and pray so that he will not fall into the temptation of placing his own comfort above what he knows to be right. And with that, Jesus leaves and prays to God for a second time, but this time, he fully commits himself to what he knows God is calling him to do; he says something like, "I am afraid and wish I did not have to do this. But if it is the only way, then so be it, I will just have to be afraid." And as soon as Jesus finishes his prayer, the authorities show up and arrest him, causing all of his loyal followers to abandon him and run away in terror.[300]

In the dark of the night, Jesus is taken to an assembly of elders, high priests, and teachers of the law, where he is put on trial and found guilty of blasphemy—a crime worthy of death.[301] And once this verdict is reached, the Pharisees hand Jesus over to the Romans to be beaten, humiliated, and nailed to a cross. And as he hangs there slowly dying, Jesus cries out in a loud voice, "My God, My God, why have you forsaken me?"[302] a line that can hardly be overlooked. In his darkest moment, Jesus looks up to the sky and says something like, "I did everything right, everything I was supposed to do . . . *Where are you?!*" Here is a man who doesn't understand why things have turned out the way that they have, and in his greatest moment of need, feels like even God Himself has turned His back and abandoned him.[303] And despite all of this—despite having done nothing wrong, having been betrayed and abandoned by his closest friends, having been humiliated, beaten, and executed by his enemies, plagued with doubt about the goodness of Being, and feeling like even God Himself has deserted him—Jesus *still* chooses to have faith; still chooses to value God, truth, and love above all things; still chooses to fully commit himself to what he knows God is calling him to do. And with his dying breath, Jesus calls out one last time, "Father, into your hands I commit my spirit."[304]

The story of Jesus ends with Jesus being placed inside of a tomb and after three days, resurrecting from the dead. And once resurrected, Jesus appears to his disciples and tells them that it is now their responsibility to spread the word of his teaching—to spread the good news—and make believers of the world.[305] And after giving his disciples these final instructions, Jesus ascends to heaven and sits at the right hand of God.[306]

## The Good News

An important part of Christian theology is sharing the good news—the story of Jesus Christ—with the rest of the world, a story that can be summarized quite nicely with a single Bible verse:

> "For God so loved the world that he gave his one and only Son, that whoever believes in him shall not perish but have eternal life." (John 3:16)

But what does this verse mean exactly? For starters, we already know the kingdom of God is a place that we experience within the world of meaning, and eternal life is a type of life that will nourish our souls and give us the meaning and purpose necessary to face the tragedy of existence and prevail. And so the good news states that if we believe in Jesus, then we will be able to enter into this kingdom and receive an eternally fulfilling life. Which then begs the question: what does it actually mean to *believe* in Jesus? It's fairly common for people to define belief as something akin to intellectual thought, that if we *think* the story of Jesus actually occurred in history, then that means we believe in him. But consider this: if we have zero conviction for an idea—that is, if an idea has no effect on how we actually live in the world—then in what way can we reasonably claim to *believe* that idea?

Nietzsche believed that Paul, and later the Protestants following Luther, had removed moral responsibility from Christ's followers. They had watered down the idea of *the imitation of Christ*. This imitation was the sacred duty of the believer not to adhere (or merely to mouth) a set of statements about abstract belief but instead to actually manifest the spirit of the Saviour in the particular, specific conditions of his or her life—to realize or incarnate the archetype, as Jung had it; to clothe the eternal pattern in flesh. Nietzsche writes, "The Christians have never practiced the actions Jesus prescribed them; and the impudent garrulous talk about the 'justification by faith' and its supreme and sole significance is only the consequence of the Church's lack of courage and will to profess the works Jesus demanded." Nietzsche was, indeed, a critic without parallel.

Dogmatic belief in the central axioms of Christianity (that Christ's crucifixion redeemed the world; that salvation was reserved for the hereafter; that salvation could not be achieved through works) had three mutually reinforcing consequences: First, *devaluation of the significance of earthly life, as only the here-after mattered*. This also meant that it had become acceptable to overlook and shirk responsibility for the suffering that existed in the here-and-now; Second, *passive acceptance of the status quo, because salvation could not be earned in any case through effort in this life* . . . and, finally, third, *the right of the believer to reject any real moral burden* (outside of the stated belief in salvation through Christ), *because the Son of God had already done all the important work*. It was for such reasons that Dostoevsky, who was a great influence on Nietzsche, also criticized institutional Christianity (although he arguably managed it in a more ambiguous but also more sophisticated manner). In his masterwork, *The Brothers Karamazov*, Dostoevsky has his atheist superman, Ivan, tell a little story, "The Grand Inquisitor." A brief review is in order.

Ivan speaks to his brother Alyosha—whose pursuits as a monastic novitiate he holds in contempt—of Christ returning to Earth at the time of the Spanish Inquisition. The returning Savior makes quite a ruckus, as would be expected. He heals the sick. He raises the dead. His antics soon attract attention from the Grand Inquisitor himself, who promptly has Christ arrested and thrown into a prison cell. Later, the Inquisitor pays Him a visit. He informs Christ that he is no longer needed. His return is simply too great a threat to the Church. The Inquisitor tells Christ that the burden He laid on mankind—the burden of existence in faith and truth—was simply too great for mere mortals to bear. The inquisitor claims that the Church, in its mercy, diluted that message, lifting the demand for perfect Being from the shoulders of its followers, providing them instead with the simple and merciful escapes of faith and the afterlife. That work took centuries, says the Inquisitor, and the last thing the church needs after all that effort is the return of the Man who insisted that people bear all the weight in the first place. Christ listens in silence. Then, as the Inquisitor turns to leave, Christ embraces him, and kisses him on the lips. The Inquisitor turns white, in shock. Then he goes out, leaving the cell door open.[307]

Both Nietzsche and Dostoevsky believed the church robbed people of their responsibility to live as Christ lived by insisting that eternal life could be achieved through faith alone—through thinking and stating belief without requiring any works. But it is important to note, at its most fundamental level, true faith cannot be separated from works because true faith requires conviction, and conviction inevitably results in action.

What good is it, my brothers, if a man claims to have faith but has no deeds? Can such faith save him? Suppose a brother or a sister is without clothes and daily food. If one of you says to him, "Go, I wish you well; keep warm and well fed," but does nothing about his physical needs, what good is it? In the same way, faith by itself, if not accompanied by action, is dead.

But someone will say, "You have faith; I have deeds."

Show me your faith without deeds, and I will show you my faith by what I do. You believe that there is one God. Good! Even the demons believe that—and shudder.

You foolish man, do you want evidence that faith without deeds is useless? Was not our ancestor Abraham considered righteous for what he did when he offered his son Isaac on the altar? You see that his faith and his actions were working together, and his faith was made complete by what he did. And the scripture was fulfilled that says, "Abraham believed God, and it was credited to him as righteousness," and he was called God's friend. You see that a person is justified by what he does and not by faith alone.

In the same way, was not even Rahab the prostitute considered righteous for what she did when she gave lodging to the spies and sent them off in a different direction? As the body without the spirit is dead, so faith without deeds is dead. (James 2:14)

To believe in Jesus means something far greater than to think or say the words, "I believe in Jesus;" to believe in Jesus means to live a certain way, to have faith in his teachings—to put our trust in God—and then to act that faith out in the world.

"Not everyone who says to me, 'Lord, Lord,' will enter the kingdom of heaven, but only he who does the will of my Father who is in heaven." (Matthew 7:21)

To believe in Jesus is to put his teachings into practice and to live as he lived.

Jesus answered, "I am the way and the truth and the life. No one comes to the Father except through me." (John 14:6)

To believe in Jesus is to embody the hero; it is to strive to make things better instead of worse; it is to value God, truth, and love above all things despite how unfairly we feel we are being treated by life. It is to pay attention and to do what we know to be right; to hear what God is calling us to do and then to sacrifice ourselves to that call. This is the hypothesis of the West, the good news: that if we embody Jesus—if we choose to place God above all things and sacrifice our own selfish desires for what we know to be right—then we will enter into the kingdom of God and receive a meaning and a purpose so fulfilling that we will be able to face the tragedy of existence and prevail.

Then Jesus said to his disciples, "If anyone would come after me, he must deny himself and take up his cross and follow me. For whoever wants to save his life will lose it, but whoever loses his life for me will find it. What good will it be for a man if he gains the whole world, yet forfeits his soul? (Matthew 16:24–26)

**"The New Testament is quite interesting because all of a sudden you're supposed to act as if God is nothing but good. That's such a strange thing because you look at the world and you think, 'Yeah, really? Just good, eh?' The cancer and the earthquakes are kind of hard to fit into that picture, and the terrible things that happen to children is very difficult to square with the notion of a good God. But the underlying idea is *if you act in that manner, then it makes it more likely to be true.* It's something like that. I would consider it an act of both courage and faith. You're going to make the case— like God makes at the beginning of the Bible—that Being is in fact good . . . It's a metaphysical presupposition. It's a decision to act that way . . . There's a courageous element to it which I think is also expressed in Christ's voluntary sacrifice of his own life. His presupposition was something like: I'm going to act as if God is good, and I'm going to play that out right to the end.**[308]**

**"And so the paradoxical injunction here is to accept responsibility for the catastrophe of your life, and that way you transcend it simultaneously. There's an unbelievably hopeful message in there, and the message is: you're actually**

**strong enough to do that, you just don't know it. You won't find out until you do it; you *can't* find out until you do it. . . . It's a massive risk. It's the ultimate risk. You have to be willing to lose your life in order to find it."[309]**

According to the book of Genesis, mankind was created in the image and likeness of God, but as soon as we placed our own selfish desires above what we knew to be right, we rejected this likeness and were kicked out of paradise. Now the apostle Paul, a leader of the early Christian church, wrote a letter to the Christians of Colossae in Asia Minor where he refers to Jesus as "the *image* of the invisible God."[310] Like Adam, Jesus was created in the image of God, but whereas Adam chose to hide from God's call, Jesus chose to embrace what he was being called to do. Perhaps this means that Jesus was the first man to truly embody the image of God; the first man to fully embody the logos—truth motivated by love—and therefore, live up to what God had initially envisioned man to be. And perhaps this also means that if we could sacrifice ourselves to what God is calling us to do—that is, if we could truly believe in Jesus—then we too could live up to our potential as images of God and return to paradise.

The character of Jesus has roots that reach back to the beginning of our species and represents a way of living that will allow us to overcome the tragedy of life. Christ is not only an external figure, but he is an internal figure as well, an internal possibility lying dormant within all of us. He is the manifestation of ultimate human possibility, and a representation of everything we could be if we lived up to our highest potential. And it is ultimately up to us, according to the Christian doctrine, to try and manifest this internal possibility in the external world. Only then will we be able to experience meaning so revitalizing that it will be possible to transcend our suffering and enter into God's kingdom.

**"You can think about Christ from a psychological perspective, and this particular critic I have been reading said, 'Well that doesn't differentiate Christ much from a whole sequence of dying and resurrecting mythological gods.' . . . The difference between those mythological gods and Christ is that there's**

also a historical representation of Christ's existence as well . . . And so what you have in the figure of Christ is an actual person who actually lived, plus a myth (and in some sense Christ is the union of those two things). . . . I've seen sometimes the objective world and the narrative world touch—that's *Jungian synchronicity.* I've seen that many times in my own life and so, in some sense, I believe it is undeniable. We have a narrative sense of the world. For me that's been the world of morality [the world of meaning]—that's the world that tells us how to act. It's real; we treat it like it's real. It's not the objective world. But the narrative and the objective world can touch. And the ultimate example of that in principle is supposed to be Christ. That seems to me oddly plausible. I still don't know what to make of it. Partly because it's too terrifying a reality to fully believe. I don't even know what would happen to you if you fully believed it."[311]

What would our lives look like if we chose to become the hero of our own story; if we chose to truly believe in Jesus, and devoted ourselves to the service of God? The character of Christ is the archetypal hero who lies dormant within each of us. And maybe if we could manifest this internal figure within our own lives, then we could bridge the gap between the material world of objects and the spiritual world of meaning—allowing the divine force of Love that exists within the world of meaning to take on material form and express itself in the physical world—and as a result, truly experience the kingdom of God and receive everlasting life. It's a crazy thought, but perhaps it is not impossible. In fact, what if it has already been done before? Just once. By one man . . . Now wouldn't that be something?

## Recap

- The hero of our culture is Jesus Christ.
- Baptism is a symbolic representation of repentance; it is the decision to change the direction of one's life by choosing to value God—love, truth, and making things better—above all things.
- After being baptized, Jesus is led into the desert where he overcomes

the three most fundamental temptations we all face in life: (1) to value survival over spiritual growth, (2) to doubt our importance and what we are being called to do, (3) and to place our own selfish desires above what we know to be right.

- Jesus sets out to teach people about the kingdom of God. The kingdom of God is a place where we experience eternal life, a type of life that exists within the world of meaning and fills us with the purpose and strength necessary to face the tragedy of existence and prevail.

- According to Jesus, the steps for reaching the kingdom of God are to: (1) value God above all things, (2) have faith in what we are being called to do, (3) and then act on that faith.

- The Pharisees and teachers of the law represent the Tyrannical Father who suffocates his own sons. Jesus is the hero who places spirit over dogma, the hero who travels to the underworld, and gives blind tradition sight.

- Although Jesus does not understand why things are happening the way they are, he still chooses to have faith; he still chooses to value God above all things and sacrifice himself to love, truth, and making things better.

- The good news of Christianity states that whoever believes in Jesus—whoever embodies the personality of Christ and chooses to live as he lived—will receive eternal life.

CHAPTER FIFTEEN

# Discovering Our Purpose

*What is the meaning of life?*

DISCOVERING THE PURPOSE OF OUR lives is one of the most important things we could ever do. Purpose not only gives our lives meaning, but it also gives us the strength necessary to embrace our suffering and carry on. But how do we discover our purpose? Viktor Frankl attempts to answer this question in his book, *Man's Search For Meaning*:

> As we said before, any attempt to restore a man's inner strength in the [concentration] camp had first to succeed in showing him some future goal. Nietzsche's words, "He who has a *why* to live for can bear with almost any *how*," could be the guiding motto for all psychotherapeutic and psychohygienic efforts regarding prisoners. Whenever there was an opportunity for it, one had to give them a why—an aim—for their lives, in order to strengthen them to bear the terrible *how* of their existence. Woe to him who saw no more sense in his life, no aim, no purpose, and therefore no point in carrying on. He was soon lost. The typical reply with which such a man rejected all encouraging arguments was, "I have nothing to expect from life any more." What sort of answer can one give to that?

What was really needed was a fundamental change in our attitude toward life. We had to learn ourselves and, furthermore, we had to teach the despairing men, that *it did not really matter what we expected from life, but rather what life expected from us.* We needed to stop asking about the meaning of life, and instead to think of ourselves as those who were being questioned by life—daily and hourly. Our answer must consist, not in talk and meditation, but in right action and in right conduct. Life ultimately means taking the responsibility to find the right answer to its problems and to fulfill the tasks which it constantly sets for each individual.

These tasks, and therefore the meaning of life, differ from man to man, and from moment to moment. Thus it is impossible to define the meaning of life in a general way. Questions about the meaning of life can never be answered by sweeping statements. "Life" does not mean something vague, but something very real and concrete, just as life's tasks are also very real and concrete.[312]

Ultimately, Frankl believed that we were asking the wrong questions—instead of asking something of life, he thought that we should reverse the question and recognize that it is we who are being asked. Or said another way, instead of demanding something from life, Frankl thought that we should ask, "What is life demanding of *me*? What is God calling *me* to do?"

Remember, we each have something unique calling to us—our own personal snitch to chase—and therefore the meaning of life will not be the same for everyone, but rather, it will be something unique to each individual.[313] Frankl continues:

I doubt whether a doctor can answer this question in general terms. For the meaning of life differs from man to man, from day to day and from hour to hour. What matters, therefore, is not the meaning of life in general but rather the specific meaning of a person's life at a given moment. To put the questions in general terms would be comparable to the question posed to a chess champion: "Tell me, Master, what is the best move in the world?" There simply is no such thing as the best or even a good move apart from the particular situation in a game and the particular personality of one's opponent. The same holds for human existence. One should not search for an abstract meaning of life. Everyone has his own specific vocation or mission in life to carry out a concrete assignment which demands fulfillment. Therein he cannot be replaced nor can his life be repeated. Thus, everyone's task is as unique as is his specific opportunity to implement it . . .[314]

I remember two cases of would-be suicide, which bore a striking similarity to each other. Both men had talked of their intentions to commit suicide. Both used the typical argument—they had nothing more to expect from life. In both cases it was a question of getting them to realize that life was still expecting something from them; something in the future was expected of them. We found, in fact, that for the one it was his child whom he adored and who was waiting for him in a foreign country. For the other it was a thing, not a person. This man was a scientist and had written a series of books which still needed to be finished. His work could not be done by anyone else, any more than another person could ever take the place of the father in his child's affections.

This uniqueness and singleness which distinguishes each individual and gives a meaning to his existence has a bearing on creative work as much as it does on human love. When the impossibility of replacing a person is realized, it allows the responsibility which a man has for his existence and its continuance to appear in all its magnitude. A man who becomes conscious of the responsibility he bears toward a human being who affectionately waits for him, or to an unfinished work, will never be able to throw away his life. He knows the "why" for his existence, and will be able to bear almost any "how."[315]

Frankl goes on to note that meaning is not actually something we can directly pursue, but rather, something that must come about organically. In an attempt to explain this idea further, he compares the pursuit of meaning to something like the pursuit of laughter. Genuine laugher is not something we can force, but instead, happens naturally whenever we are provided with a *reason* to laugh (e.g., someone tells us a joke).[316] Likewise, meaning is a symptom that only manifests as a result of some genuine pursuit, a side effect that can only be experienced by *actively doing something in the world.*

Now remember, according to Genesis, God created man with a built-in purpose: to make things better by furthering His creation. And believe it or not, this is essentially the same idea posited by Viktor Frankl—Frankl believed that everyone had a purpose, that our purpose was unique and personal to us, and that it revolved around *doing* something in the world, i.e., some act of *furthering creation.* Now according to Frankl, an "act of furthering creation" is not necessarily limited to something physical, but rather, can be anything from:

1. Creating a work or doing a deed
2. Experiencing something (goodness, truth, and beauty) or encountering someone (caring for, or loving someone)
3. The attitude that one chooses to take towards unavoidable suffering (transforming a personal tragedy into a triumph)[317]

And after Genesis tells us that man's purpose is to further creation, we are then taught how to actually do that in the gospels, how to actually find our purpose and become images of God:

1. Choose to value God—love, truth, and making things better—above all things
2. Ask what life is expecting of us and what God is calling us to do
3. Pay attention to what God is calling us to do
4. Have faith in what we are being called to do, and then sacrifice ourselves to that call despite the temptation to do otherwise

If we do this successfully, then we will have found our "why" that can overcome any "how"; we will have discovered our life's purpose and, as a result, will have encountered a meaning so fulfilling that we will consider the suffering in our lives a reasonable price to pay.

Interestingly enough, these steps also seem to be what ultimately led to the creation of Frankl's book:

The reader may ask me why I did not try to escape what was in store for me after Hitler had occupied Austria. Let me answer by recalling the following story. Shortly before the United States entered World War II, I received an invitation to come to the American Consulate in Vienna to pick up my immigration visa. My old parents were overjoyed because they expected that I would soon be allowed to leave Austria. I suddenly hesitated, however. The question beset me: could I really afford to leave my parents alone to face their fate, to be sent, sooner or later, to a concentration camp, or even to a so-called extermination camp? Where did my responsibility lie? Should I foster my brain child, logotherapy, by emigrating to fertile soil where I could write my books? Or should I concentrate on my duties as a real child, the child of my parents who had to do whatever he could to protect them? I pondered the problem this way and that but could not arrive at a solution; this was the type of dilemma that made one wish for "a hint from Heaven," as the phrase goes.

It was then that I noticed a piece of marble lying on a table at home. When I asked my father about it, he explained that he had found it on the site where the National Socialists had burned down the largest Viennese synagogue. He had taken the piece home because it was a part of the tablets on which the Ten Commandments were inscribed. One gilded Hebrew letter was engraved on the piece; my father explained that this letter stood for one of the Commandments. Eagerly I asked, "Which one is it?" He answered, "Honor thy father and thy mother that thy days may be long upon the land." At that moment I decided to stay with my father and my mother upon the land, and to let the American visa lapse.[318]

During World War II, Viktor Frankl had the opportunity to leave Austria and pursue writing his book, but something about that felt wrong to him. He then asked for a "hint from Heaven"—that is, he asked what life was expecting of him—and as a result, it became exceedingly clear to him what he was being called to do.

Upon hearing the call of God, Frankl chose to have faith, and to sacrifice himself for what he knew to be right by staying with his parents and allowing his visa to lapse. Frankl entered the concentration camp alongside his parents, wife, and life's work, and returned home with nothing; enough to make any man question why they had been forsaken by God. But despite how things appeared, Frankl continued to have faith, and while in camp, found a purpose for his suffering, a reason to continue—Frankl chose to use his experience in the concentration camp as a way to further develop the ideas presented in his book. And as a result of his experience, *Man's Search for Meaning* has positively impacted the lives of millions of people around the world today, something which some might consider to be a modern-day miracle.

We currently have a bad habit of only looking at the world through a scientific lens. But the problem is that the scientific lens can only see the world of objects, and our life's purpose can only be found within the world of meaning. You see, the scientific lens trains people to see the world without any meaning, but this is simply an intellectual trick, as anything can be rendered meaningless if looked at from a certain angle. The truth is that life is meaningful, and we know that it is meaningful because we experience that meaning every day; it is only later that we attempt to talk ourselves out of this meaning because we cannot make sense of it scientifically. Therefore, moving forward, we should change how we think about such things; if we are viewing the world in a way that makes us feel like life has no meaning, the answer is not that life is meaningless, but that we are viewing the world with the wrong lens.

**"No one stops listening to a symphony because they know it is going to end . . . You can pick a timeframe of evaluation that makes all your efforts futile . . . It's like 'What's the point of stopping this baby from crying when the sun is going to envelop the Earth in four billion years?' . . . You know that's preposterous! But why? That's the existential question, right? If we are all doomed to ashes and decay, why do anything?**

I used the baby crying example for a reason—who in the world is going to use that argument to not feed their baby? Well, why feed that thing? In four billion years the sun is going to envelop the Earth! It's like *wrong timeframe, folks!* . . . If you are adopting a timeframe that makes what you are doing appear trivial, the problem isn't necessarily what you are doing . . . the problem is that your mind, which is capable of leaping across evaluative frameworks, has picked a timeframe inappropriate for the task. So quit doing that! Instead, why don't you practice adopting the timeframe that imbues your properly oriented action with the deepest possible apprehended meaning . . . I would say that's a profound neurophysiological signal that you're in the right place at the right time because it's accompanied by a sense of deep wellbeing, and that's literally an antidote to suffering . . . The question is, how is that best to be found? Well that's an empirical question. You have to look in your own life and see where meaning glimmers and then pursue that."[319]

Life is meaningful, and the meanings we experience are undeniably real. As a species, we have an instinct for meaning, and this instinct seems to work as an orienting reflex that guides us towards our life's purpose.[320] And if we allow this instinct to guide us—if we do what we know to be right and sacrifice ourselves to what we are being called to do—then we will soon discover our purpose, and as a result, experience that life-sustaining meaning that comes along with it.

Interest is a spirit beckoning from the unknown, a spirit calling from outside the "walls" of society. Pursuit of individual interest means hearkening to this spirit's call, journeying outside the protective walls of childhood dependence and adolescent group identification, and returning to rejuvenate society. This means that pursuit of individual interest—development of true individuality—is equivalent to identification with the hero. Such identification renders the world bearable, despite its tragedies, and reduces neurotic suffering, which destroys faith, to an absolute minimum.

This is the message that everyone wants to hear. Risk your security. Face the unknown. Quit lying to yourself, and do what your heart truly tells you to do. You will be better for it, and so will the world.[321]

## Recap

- We must stop asking *what is the meaning of life* and instead realize that it is *we* who are being asked. Instead of expecting something from life, we should ask *what is life expecting from me?*
- Meaning is not something we can directly pursue, but rather, something that must come about organically; it is a symptom of actively doing something in the world.
- According to Frankl, our life's purpose will be unique to us and revolve around doing something in the world. Examples of this might be anything from:

    1. Creating a work or doing a deed
    2. Experiencing something or loving someone
    3. The attitude we take towards unavoidable suffering

- According to Genesis, God created man with a built-in purpose: to make things better by furthering His creation. And according to the gospels, furthering creation can only be accomplished by:

    1. Choosing to value God above all things
    2. Asking what life is expecting of us and what God is calling us to do
    3. Paying attention to what God is calling us to do
    4. Having faith in what we are being called to do and sacrificing ourselves to that call

- Our life's purpose exists within the world of meaning, and in order to discover this purpose, we must first value God above all things, and then allow our instinct for meaning to guide us.

# CHAPTER SIXTEEN

# The World of Meaning

THERE ARE SOME THINGS IN the world that are extremely tangible and easy to define, and therefore everyone agrees that they exist. But what about those things that are less tangible; those things that are harder to define and cause a considerable amount of debate and disagreement—how can we know whether or not *those* things exist?

There is an approach in psychology called the *multitrait-multimethod matrix*, and this approach is used to indicate the existence of things that are not easily measured. The idea behind this approach is that if we can measure a phenomenon using multiple techniques and draw the same conclusion, then it is reasonable to assume that this phenomenon actually exists (sort of like how our five senses work together to indicate the nature of something).[322]

Now, in a sense, we have been using the multitrait-multimethod matrix throughout the entirety of this book in an attempt to validate the ideas we have been discussing. So far, we have discussed these ideas in terms of:

1. Philosophy
2. Cognitive psychology, as well as some neuropsychology
3. Narrative and mythology
4. Cross-cultural manifestations—how the same ideas are prevalent among many different cultures

When we view the ideas presented in this book across these different levels of analysis, we begin to see a pattern emerge—a pattern that becomes increasingly less likely to exist the more techniques we use to examine it and, therefore, may be an indication of something real.[323]

The world is a very weird and complicated place, and as a species, our perceptions of the world are very limited. Therefore, isn't it entirely possible that there are things happening all around us that we cannot understand? Frankl elaborates:

> After a while I proceeded to another question, this time addressing myself to the whole group. The question was whether an ape which was being used to develop poliomyelitis serum, and for this reason punctured again and again, would ever be able to grasp the meaning of its suffering. Unanimously, the group replied that of course it would not; with its limited intelligence, it could not enter into the world of man, i.e., the only world in which the meaning of its suffering would be understandable. Then I pushed forward with the following question: "And what about man? Are you sure that the human world is a terminal point in the evolution of the cosmos? Is it not conceivable that there is still another dimension, a world beyond man's world; a world in which the question of an ultimate meaning of human suffering would find an answer?[324]

Is it not possible there could be a fourth dimension that interacts with our three-dimensional world; a realm containing the world of meaning that we cannot directly perceive but might be able to infer? For example, imagine that we drew a stick figure on a piece of paper. Now imagine taking a ball, dipping that ball in paint, and touching that ball to the same piece of paper, leaving behind a paint splotch. Essentially, this is what it looks like when a three-dimensional object (a ball) comes into contact with a two-dimensional space (a piece of paper). Because our stick figure does not have the ability to perceive three-dimensional objects, when the ball touches the piece of paper, he will not perceive a three-dimensional ball but rather a two-dimensional image (the paint splotch). That is, our stick figure will see *a pattern* indicating the ball's existence within a higher dimension.

Figure 16.1

So although our stick figure cannot perceive this ball directly, he can infer its existence and perhaps even represent it to others using those patterns he can perceive.

Likewise, if a fourth dimension did exist, it would be impossible for us to perceive it directly; it would be a place that transcends all reason and logic, a place we could only point to as a result of witnessing its shadows.

Just like a two-dimensional stick figure interacting with a three-dimensional ball, whenever something from a higher dimension comes into contact with a lower dimension, those who exist within that lower dimension will only be able to perceive an altered image of what is truly there—that is, a pattern indicating the existence of something higher. Now, when we look at the stories mankind has produced over time, there seems to be two fundamental patterns that consistently manifest within these stories, patterns that represent two fundamental forces operating within our world—that is, the forces of good and evil. And although we cannot directly measure these two forces scientifically, we can infer their existence by the patterns they produce. But remember, what we are witnessing are only patterns—altered images of what is actually there—and therefore, should not be confused with the actual forces themselves.

**Fig. 16.1**[325] shows a famous painting by artist René Magritte captioned "This is not a pipe." So what does this painting mean exactly? What idea was Magritte trying to communicate through this piece of art? Well, ask yourself this: when you look at this image, are you actually looking at a pipe, or are you looking at a *picture* of a pipe? This painting is an attempt by Magritte to show how symbols should not be confused with the things they represent, for a map is not the actual territory any more than a menu is real food.[326]

As a species, we looked at the world and saw patterns indicating the existence of something higher. We then began to symbolically represent these patterns through stories. But as soon as we began telling stories about the patterns of God, we began to confuse the symbols of God for the Almighty Himself.[327] And over time, once we had fully developed our scientific view of the world, we destroyed these symbols and arrogantly believed it was God we had destroyed. But we did no such thing, for we merely destroyed a symbol that was used to represent a two-dimensional paint splotch and, in our infinite wisdom, believed we had destroyed a three-dimensional ball. God is not dead; His symbols simply need reviving.

There seems to be another world that exists outside of the material world, a world that we experience and treat as our primary reality. But because we cannot explain this world scientifically, we pretend that it's not real; we pretend it is an illusion only the unenlightened can see. But make no mistake, the spiritual world is real, it is just a different type of real than we are use to.

As humans, we live in the midst of two dimensions—the material world of objects and the spiritual world of meaning—and it appears we are what unites these two worlds together. The story of the West tells us that man is a manifestation of these two worlds, and how we choose to bring them together actually matters. It is a story that claims we have a purpose—to make things better by furthering creation—and how this purpose plays itself out in the particulars is unique to each individual; that if we choose to value God above all things, have faith in what we are being called to do, and sacrifice ourselves to that call, then we will successfully bridge the gap between these two worlds and ultimately overcome the tragedy of life, ascend to heaven, and sit at the right hand of God. But the catch is, we won't know if this is true unless we try it, unless we sacrifice our entire lives to this pursuit. It is the ultimate sacrifice, the ultimate act of faith. We must be willing to lose our lives in order to find them.

## Recap

- We have used the multitrait-multimethod approach to validate the ideas presented in this book.
- When a higher dimension comes into contact with a lower dimension it is perceived as an altered image—that is, *a pattern*.
- When we look at the stories mankind has produced over time, there seems to be two fundamental patterns that consistently manifest within these stories, patterns that represent two fundamental forces operating within our world—the forces of good and evil.
- Once we developed symbols to represent the patterns we saw in the world, we immediately confused these symbols for the transcendent

phenomena they were supposed to be representing. And once we had fully developed our scientific lens, we then destroyed these symbols and arrogantly believed it was God we had destroyed.

• Our ancestors used stories to symbolically represent the patterns they saw in the world. These stories insist we have a purpose—to make things better by furthering creation; they claim that if we choose to value God above all things, have faith in what we are being called to do, and sacrifice ourselves to that call, then we will successfully bridge the gap between these two worlds, and ultimately overcome the tragedy of life, ascend to heaven, and sit at the right hand of God.

# Part Three Recap

## In The Beginning

In the book of Genesis, God created order out of chaos using the logos—truthful speech motivated by love. He then created man in His likeness, which means that men and women also have the ability to create order out of chaos using the logos. And once God created man, he then endowed us with a purpose—*to make things better by furthering His creation.*

## East of Eden

The story of Cain and Abel is a foundational story of Western civilization. It is a story that says there are two forces operating in the human psyche that can be conceptualized as brothers who are murderously opposed to one another, and that it is ultimately up to each individual to choose which personality they will manifest. The Bible portrays Noah as a man who chose to embody the personality of Abel instead of the personality of Cain, and as a result, was able to hear the call of God and save humanity from destruction.

## The Good News

Jesus Christ is the hero of our culture and represents the West's hypothesis on how we should live in the world. Fundamentally, the hypothesis of the West is this: that if we believe in Jesus—if we choose to embody the personality of Christ and live as he lived—then we will find our purpose and receive a meaning so fulfilling that we will be able to transcend the tragedy of our lives.

## Discovering Our Purpose

Meaning is not something that can be pursued, but rather, it must come as a result of actively doing something in the world. Genesis states that man's purpose—our purpose—is to make things better by further creation, and Jesus is the shinning exemplar of how to do this:

1.  Choose to value God above all things
2.  Ask what God is calling us to do
3.  Pay attention to what God is calling us to do
4.  Have faith in what we are being called to do, and sacrifice ourselves to that call

The gospels indicate that these four steps—which outline how to follow Jesus—are the path to reaching the kingdom of God.

## The World of Meaning

It is possible that there is a fourth dimension that interacts with our three-dimensional world; a realm containing the world of meaning that we cannot directly perceive but might be able to infer. When we look at the stories mankind has produced, there seems to be two fundamental patterns that consistently manifest within these stories, patterns that represent two fundamental forces operating within our world—the forces of good and evil. We represented these patterns with symbols, but then confused these symbols for the real thing. And so, when we destroyed these symbols on scientific grounds, we thought we had killed God. But we did no such thing, we merely destroyed the symbols that were being used to represent God. God is not dead; His symbols simply need reviving.

Now what I am commanding you today is not too difficult for you or beyond your reach. It is not up in heaven, so that you have to ask, "Who will ascend into heaven to get it and proclaim it to us so we may obey it?" Nor is it beyond the sea, so that you have to ask, "Who will cross the sea to get it and proclaim it to us so we may obey it?" No, the word is very near you; it is in your mouth and in your heart so you may obey it.

See, I set before you today life and prosperity, death and destruction. For I command you today to love the LORD your God, to walk in his ways, and to keep his commands, decrees and laws; then you will live and increase, and the LORD your God will bless you in the land you are entering to possess.

But if your heart turns away and you are not obedient, and if you are drawn away to bow down to other gods and worship them, I declare to you this day that you will certainly be destroyed. You will not live long in the land you are crossing the Jordan to enter and possess.

This day I call the heavens and the earth as witnesses against you that I have set before you life and death, blessings and curses. Now choose life, so that you and your children may live and that you may love the LORD your God, listen to his voice, and hold fast to him. For the LORD is your life, and he will give you many years in the land he swore to give to your fathers, Abraham, Isaac and Jacob.

(Deuteronomy 30:11–20)

# Sources

1. 2017 Personality and Transformations Lecture 10: Humanism & Phen: Carl Rogers
   https://www.youtube.com/watch?v=68tFnjkIZ1Q&list=PL22J3Va
   eABQApSdW8X71Ihe34eKN6XhCi&index=8.

2. 2017 Personality and Transformations Lecture 12: Heidigger, Ben and Boss
   https://www.youtube.com/watch?v=11oBFCNeTAs&list=PL22J3V
   aeABQApSdW8X71Ihe34eKN6XhCi&index=10.

3. 2016 Personality Lecture 07: Phenomenology and Carl Rogers
   https://www.youtube.com/watch?v=3uJkd54p9dY&list=PL22J3Va
   eABQAOhH1CLMNnMl2R-O1abW1T&index=7.

4. 2016 Lecture 09: phenomenology
   https://www.youtube.com/watch?v=539UQF6eT6I&list=PL22J3V
   aeABQAOhH1CLMNnMl2R-O1abW1T&index=9.

5. 2014 Personality Lecture 12: Binswanger & Boss (Phenomenology)
   https://www.youtube.com/watch?v=UzdpzuEkL74&list=PL22J3Vae
   ABQCfQy9Yg2y8fi5cI8HYUUct&index=10.

6. 2015 Personality Lecture 10: Humanism: Carl Rogers
   https://www.youtube.com/watch?v=V9Ql5V7-
   OQo&list=PL22J3VaeABQAhrMCQUa6sde_
   Y9DVbLYRv&index=10.

7. 2014 Personality Lecture 11: Existentialism: Viktor Frankl
   https://www.youtube.com/watch?v=zooE5GE81TU&list=PL22J3V
   aeABQCfQy9Yg2y8fi5cI8HYUUct&index=9.

8. 2014 Personality Lecture 13: Aleksandr Solzhenitsyn (Existentialism)
   https://www.youtube.com/watch?v=8u3aTURVEC8&list=PL22J3V
   aeABQCfQy9Yg2y8fi5cI8HYUUct&index=11.

9. 2015 Personality Lecture 12: Existentialism: Dostoevsky, Nietzsche, Kierkegaard
https://www.youtube.com/watch?v=SsoVhKo4UvQ&list=PL22J3Vae
ABQAhrMCQUa6sde_Y9DVbLYRv&index=11.

10. 2017 Personality 11: Existentialism: Nietzsche Dostoevsky & Kierkegaard
https://www.youtube.com/watch?v=4qZ3EsrKPsc&list=PL22J3VaeA
BQApSdW8X71Ihe34eKN6XhCi&index=9.

11. Nietzsche, Dostoevsky, and The Brothers Karamazov | Jordan B Peterson
https://www.youtube.com/watch?v=KebJiLxLS5Y.

12. On Claiming Belief In God: Discussion with Dennis Prager
https://www.youtube.com/watch?v=j0GL_4cAkhI&t=299s.

13. 001 Maps of Meaning: 1 Monsters of Our Own Making (TVO)
https://www.youtube.com/watch?v=knEZN9U-9xc.

14. AA Harris/Weinstein/Peterson Discussion: Vancouver (1st night)
https://www.youtube.com/watch?v=d-Z9EZE8kpo&list=PL22J3Vae
ABQCvNnWM3p2cYMtArHCA_oWO&index=7.

15. AB Harris/Weinstein/Peterson Discussion: Vancouver (2nd night)
https://www.youtube.com/watch?v=BtkwF5qA6uE&list=PL22J3Vae
ABQCvNnWM3p2cYMtArHCA_oWO&index=8.

16. AC Harris/Murray/Peterson Discussion: Dublin
https://www.youtube.com/watch?v=ZZI-FwSQRn8&list=PL22J3Vae
ABQCvNnWM3p2cYMtArHCA_oWO&index=10.

17. AD Harris/Murray/Peterson Discussion: London
https://www.youtube.com/watch?v=YfdaAGZvYsA&list=PL22J3Vae
ABQCvNnWM3p2cYMtArHCA_oWO&index=9.

18. 2014 Personality Lecture 09: Sigmund Freud II (Depth Psychology)
https://www.youtube.com/watch?v=16WF1jLLyik&list=PL22J3VaeA
BQCfQy9Yg2y8fi5cI8HYUUct&index=7.

19. 2015 Personality Lecture 08: Depth Psychology: Sigmund Freud (Part 1)
https://www.youtube.com/watch?v=9Zji6xMkOgo&list=PL22J3Vae
ABQAhrMCQUa6sde_Y9DVbLYRv&index=8.

20. 2015 Personality Lecture 09: Depth Psychology: Sigmund Freud (Part 02)
https://www.youtube.com/watch?v=A07DV3FXyPo&list=PL22J3V
aeABQAhrMCQUa6sde_Y9DVbLYRv&index=9.

21. 2016 Personality Lecture 06: Freud: An Overview
https://www.youtube.com/watch?v=BSh37_x5RNY&list=PL22J3Vae
ABQAOhH1CLMNnMl2R-O1abW1T&index=6.

22. 2017 Personality 09: Freud and the Dynamic Unconscious
https://www.youtube.com/watch?v=YFWLwYyrMRE&list=PL22J3V
aeABQApSdW8X71Ihe34eKN6XhCi&index=7.

23. 2014 Personality Lecture 05: Jean Piaget (Constructivism)
https://www.youtube.com/watch?v=91jWsB7ZYHw&list=PL22J3Va
eABQCfQy9Yg2y8fi5cI8HYUUct&index=5.

24. 2015 Personality Lecture 05: Constructivism: Jean Piaget
https://www.youtube.com/watch?v=ED_TfmwjsEw&list=PL22J3Vae
ABQAhrMCQUa6sde_Y9DVbLYRv&index=5.

25. 2016 Personality Lecture 04: Piaget Constructivism
https://www.youtube.com/watch?v=G3fWuMQ5K8I&list=PL22J3Va
eABQAOhH1CLMNnMl2R-O1abW1T&index=4.

26. 2017 Personality 06: Jean Piaget & Constructivism
https://www.youtube.com/watch?v=BQ4VSRg4e8w&list=PL22J3Vae
ABQApSdW8X71Ihe34eKN6XhCi&index=4.

27. An Atheist in the Realm of Myth | Stephen Fry - Jordan B Peterson
Podcast - S4 E22
https://www.youtube.com/watch?v=fFFSKedy9f4.

28. 2014 Personality Lecture 06: Carl Jung (Part 1)
https://www.youtube.com/watch?v=8r8ISkQ4exM&list=PL22J3Vae
ABQCfQy9Yg2y8fi5cI8HYUUct&index=6.

29. 2015 Personality Lecture 06: Depth Psychology: Carl Jung (Part 01)
https://www.youtube.com/watch?v=DC0faZiBcG0&list=PL22J3Vae
ABQAhrMCQUa6sde_Y9DVbLYRv&index=6.

30. 2015 Personality Lecture 07: Depth Psychology: Carl Jung (Part 02)
https://www.youtube.com/watch?v=CFHZyse4VGw&list=PL22J3Va
eABQAhrMCQUa6sde_Y9DVbLYRv&index=7.

31. 2017 Personality 07: Carl Jung and the Lion King (Part 1)
https://www.youtube.com/watch?v=3iLiKMUiyTI&list=PL22J3VaeA
BQApSdW8X71Ihe34eKN6XhCi&index=5.

32. 2014 Personality Lecture 02: Mythological Representations
https://www.youtube.com/watch?v=Owgc63KhcL8&list=PL22J3Vae
ABQCfQy9Yg2y8fi5cI8HYUUct&index=2.

33. 2015 Personality Lecture 02: Historical Perspectives - Mythological Representations
https://www.youtube.com/watch?v=9fKZPRAPT1w&list=PL22J3V
aeABQAhrMCQUa6sde_Y9DVbLYRv&index=2.

34. 2017 Personality 02/03: Historical & Mythological Context
https://www.youtube.com/watch?v=HbAZ6cFxCeY&list=PL22J3V
aeABQApSdW8X71Ihe34eKN6XhCi&index=2.

35. 2014 Personality Lecture 01: Introduction and Overview
https://www.youtube.com/watch?v=_0xBOMWJkgM&list=PL22J3V
aeABQCfQy9Yg2y8fi5cI8HYUUct.

36. 2015 Personality Lecture 01: Introduction & Overview
https://www.youtube.com/watch?v=ZKpqpBRVr8Y&list=PL22J3Vae
ABQAhrMCQUa6sde_Y9DVbLYRv&index=1.

37. 2016 Personality Lecture 01: Introduction and Overview (Part 1)
https://www.youtube.com/watch?v=UGLsnu5RLe8&list=PL22J3Vae
ABQAOhH1CLMNnMl2R-O1abW1T&index=1.

38. 2016 Personality Lecture 02: Introduction and Overview (Part 2)
https://www.youtube.com/watch?v=ajtnhtEg76k&list=PL22J3VaeAB
QAOhH1CLMNnMl2R-O1abW1T&index=2.

39. 2017 Personality 01: Introduction
https://www.youtube.com/watch?v=kYYJlNbV1OM&list=PL22J3Va
eABQApSdW8X71Ihe34eKN6XhCi.

40. 2015 Maps of Meaning Lecture 01a: Introduction (Part 1)
https://www.youtube.com/watch?v=4tQOlQRp3gQ&list=PL22J3Vae
ABQByVcW4lXQ46glULC-ekhOp.

41. 2015 Maps of Meaning Lecture 1: Introduction (Part 2)
https://www.youtube.com/watch?v=rM8Jsibkr18&list=PL22J3VaeAB
QByVcW4lXQ46glULC-ekhOp&index=2.

42. 2016 Lecture 01 Maps of Meaning: Introduction and Overview
youtube.com/watch?v=bjnvtRgpg6g&list=PL22J3VaeABQAGbKJN
DrRa6GNL0iL4KoOj.

43. 2017 Maps of Meaning 01: Context and Background
https://www.youtube.com/watch?v=I8Xc2_FtpHI&list=PL22J3VaeA
BQAT-0aSPq-OKOpQlHyR4k5h&index=1.

44. 2015 Maps of Meaning Lecture 02a: Object and Meaning (Part 1)
https://www.youtube.com/watch?v=mO9LUWs5M60&list=PL22J3V
aeABQByVcW4lXQ46glULC-ekhOp&index=3.

45. 2015 Maps of Meaning Lecture 02b: Object and Meaning (Part 2)
https://www.youtube.com/watch?v=6Rd10PQVsGs&list=PL22J3Vae
ABQByVcW4lXQ46glULC-ekhOp&index=4.

46. 2016 Lecture 02 Maps of Meaning: Playable and non-playable games
https://www.youtube.com/watch?v=RcmWssTLFv0&list=PL22J3V
aeABQAGbKJNDrRa6GNL0iL4KoOj&index=2.

47. 2016 Lecture 03 Maps of Meaning: Part I: The basic story and its
transformations
https://www.youtube.com/watch?v=ux6TVYqdN-E&list=PL22J3Vae
ABQAGbKJNDrRa6GNL0iL4KoOj&index=3.

48. 2016 Lecture 03 Maps of Meaning: Part II: The basic story -- and its
transformations
https://www.youtube.com/watch?v=DmpUQEDRIKA&list=PL22J3
VaeABQAGbKJNDrRa6GNL0iL4KoOj&index=4.

49. 2017 Maps of Meaning 05: Story and Metastory (Part 1)
https://www.youtube.com/watch?v=RudKmwzDpNY&list=PL22J3V
aeABQAT-0aSPq-OKOpQlHyR4k5h&index=5.

50. 2015 Maps of Meaning Lecture 03a: Narrative, Neuropsychology &
Mythology I (Part 1)
https://www.youtube.com/watch?v=6NVY5KdSfQI&list=PL22J3Vae
ABQByVcW4lXQ46glULC-ekhOp&index=5.

51. 2015 Maps of Meaning Lecture 03b: Narrative, Neuropsychology &
Mythology I (Part 2)
https://www.youtube.com/watch?v=3nAIAPYuD7c&list=PL22J3Vae
ABQByVcW4lXQ46glULC-ekhOp&index=6.

52. 2015 Maps of Meaning 04a: Narrative, Neuropsychology & Mythology II / Part 1 (Jordan Peterson)
https://www.youtube.com/watch?v=rlGqUfIgJfc&list=PL22J3VaeAB
QByVcW4lXQ46glULC-ekhOp&index=7.

53. 2015 Maps of Meaning 04b: Narrative, Neuropsychology & Mythology II / Part 2 (Jordan Peterson)
https://www.youtube.com/watch?v=YCc-Rk1GPpQ&list=PL22J3Vae
ABQByVcW4lXQ46glULC-ekhOp&index=8.

54. 2015 Maps of Meaning 05b: Narrative, Neuropsychology & Mythology III / Part 1 (Jordan Peterson)
https://www.youtube.com/watch?v=Ov5pYNPi358&list=PL22J3Vae
ABQByVcW4lXQ46glULC-ekhOp&index=9.

55. 2016 Lecture 04 Maps of Meaning: Anomaly
    https://www.youtube.com/watch?v=DjYqkPrCvXQ&list=PL22J3Vae
    ABQAGbKJNDrRa6GNL0iL4KoOj&index=5.
56. 2016 Lecture 05: Maps of Meaning: Part I: Anomaly and the brain
    https://www.youtube.com/watch?v=ZHmklvx9oJ4&list=PL22J3Vae
    ABQAGbKJNDrRa6GNL0iL4KoOj&index=6.
57. 2016 Lecture 05 Maps of Meaning: Part II: The brain, continued
    https://www.youtube.com/watch?v=cFS6fPLQ024&list=PL22J3VaeA
    BQAGbKJNDrRa6GNL0iL4KoOj&index=7.
58. 2016 Lecture 06 Maps of Meaning: Part I: The primordial narrative
    https://www.youtube.com/watch?v=mJI0hVV-5Vs&list=PL22J3Vae
    ABQAGbKJNDrRa6GNL0iL4KoOj&index=8.
59. 2017 Maps of Meaning 06: Story and Metastory (Part 2)
    https://www.youtube.com/watch?v=nsZ8XqHPjI4&list=PL22J3VaeA
    BQAT-0aSPq-OKOpQlHyR4k5h&index=6.
60. 2017 Maps of Meaning 08: Neuropsychology of Symbolic Represen-
    tation
    https://www.youtube.com/watch?v=Nb5cBkbQpGY&list=PL22J3Va
    eABQAT-0aSPq-OKOpQlHyR4k5h&index=8'.
61. 2014 Personality Lecture 03: Heroic & Shamanic Initiations (Part 01)
    https://www.youtube.com/watch?v=iEZVWWk6qHg&list=PL22J3V
    aeABQCfQy9Yg2y8fi5cI8HYUUct&index=3.
62. 2014 Personality Lecture 04: Heroic & Shamanic Initiations (Part 02)
    https://www.youtube.com/watch?v=F9393El2Z1I&list=PL22J3VaeA
    BQCfQy9Yg2y8fi5cI8HYUUct&index=4.
63. 2015 Personality Lecture 03: Historical Perspectives - Heroic & Sha-
    manic Initiations I Mircea Eliade
    https://www.youtube.com/watch?v=t966lVrHEzo&list=PL22J3VaeA
    BQAhrMCQUa6sde_Y9DVbLYRv&index=3.
64. 2015 Personality Lecture 04: Heroic & Shamanic Initiations II: Mir-
    cea Eliade
    https://www.youtube.com/watch?v=UFAyBEKKIBE&list=PL22J3V
    aeABQAhrMCQUa6sde_Y9DVbLYRv&index=4.
65. 2016 Personality Lecture 03: Mythological Elements of the Life Story
    -- and Initiation
    https://www.youtube.com/watch?v=PH67HpFD2Ew&list=PL22J3Va
    eABQAOhH1CLMNnMl2R-O1abW1T&index=3.

66. 2017 Personality 04/05: Heroic and Shamanic Initiations https://www.youtube.com/watch?v=wLc_MC7NQek&list=PL22J3Va eABQApSdW8X71Ihe34eKN6XhCi&index=3.

67. 2015 Maps of Meaning 06a: Mythology: Introduction / Part 1 (Jordan Peterson) https://www.youtube.com/watch?v=r_ShAseOvNE&list=PL22J3Vae ABQByVcW4lXQ46glULC-ekhOp&index=11.

68. 2015 Maps of Meaning 07a: Mythology: Chaos / Part 1 (Jordan Peterson) https://www.youtube.com/watch?v=44dcUoh0oT4&list=PL22J3Vae ABQByVcW4lXQ46glULC-ekhOp&index=13.

69. 2015 Maps of Meaning 07b: Mythology: Chaos / Part 2 (Jordan Peterson) https://www.youtube.com/watch?v=rnw4SXX7cGY&list=PL22J3Vae ABQByVcW4lXQ46glULC-ekhOp&index=14.

70. 2015 Maps of Meaning 08a: Mythology: The Great Mother / Part 1 (Jordan Peterson) https://www.youtube.com/watch?v=NOzjfqO6-K8&list=PL22J3Vae ABQByVcW4lXQ46glULC-ekhOp&index=15.

71. 2015 Maps of Meaning 08b: Mythology: The Great Mother / Part 2 (Jordan Peterson) https://www.youtube.com/watch?v=w1scgquS2mo&list=PL22J3Vae ABQByVcW4lXQ46glULC-ekhOp&index=16.

72. 2015 Maps of Meaning 09a: Mythology: The Great Father / Part 1 (Jordan Peterson) https://www.youtube.com/watch?v=134BCxbMUlU&list=PL22J3Va eABQByVcW4lXQ46glULC-ekhOp&index=17.

73. 2015 Maps of Meaning 09b: Mythology: The Great Father / Part 2 (Jordan Peterson) https://www.youtube.com/watch?v=tIZb0YEcyNo&list=PL22J3VaeA BQByVcW4lXQ46glULC-ekhOp&index=18.

74. 2015 Maps of Meaning 10: Culture & Anomaly / Part 1 (Jordan Peterson) https://www.youtube.com/watch?v=Bj6HgQBNiZE&list=PL22J3Vae ABQByVcW4lXQ46glULC-ekhOp&index=19.

75. 2016 Lecture 08 Maps of Meaning: Part I: Hierarchies and chaos https://www.youtube.com/watch?v=PcYLzW1B6cY&list=PL22J3Vae ABQAGbKJNDrRa6GNL0iL4KoOj&index=12.

76. 2017 Maps of Meaning 07: Images of Story & Metastory
    https://www.youtube.com/watch?v=F3n5qtj89QE&list=PL22J3VaeA
    BQAT-0aSPq-OKOpQlHyR4k5h&index=7.
77. Tragedy vs Evil
    https://www.youtube.com/watch?v=MLp7vWB0TeY&list=PL22J3Va
    eABQBdzcPNVe0HxlPvNEEr7p5b&index=4.
78. A Change of Heart Towards Jordan | Africa Brooke | Mikhaila Peter-
    son Podcast | #120
    https://www.youtube.com/watch?v=v8v7ueICWuU\.
79. 2015 Maps of Meaning 05b: Mythology: Enuma Elish / Part 2 (Jor-
    dan Peterson)
    https://www.youtube.com/watch?v=VJVMtUb-LEY&list=PL22J3Vae
    ABQByVcW4lXQ46glULC-ekhOp&index=10.
80. 2016 Lecture 06 Maps of Meaning: Part II: The Primordial Narrative
    continued
    https://www.youtube.com/watch?v=5Q_GIHDpuZw&list=PL22J3Va
    eABQAGbKJNDrRa6GNL0iL4KoOj&index=9.
81. The Enuma Elish
    https://www.worldhistory.org/article/225/enuma-elish---the-babylo
    nian-epic-of-creation---fu/.
82. 2015 Maps of Meaning 06b: Mythology: Egyptian Myths / Part 2
    (Jordan Peterson)
    https://www.youtube.com/watch?v=aI-pET9YD6A&list=PL22J3Vae
    ABQByVcW4lXQ46glULC-ekhOp&index=12.
83. 2016 Lecture 07 Maps of Meaning: Part I: Osiris, Set, Isis and
    Horus
    https://www.youtube.com/watch?v=HueFqvz1oDU&list=PL22J3Vae
    ABQAGbKJNDrRa6GNL0iL4KoOj&index=10.
84. 2016 Lecture 07 Maps of Meaning: Part II: Osiris, Set, Isis and Horus
    https://www.youtube.com/watch?v=sta4zLcTAII&list=PL22J3Vae
    ABQAGbKJNDrRa6GNL0iL4KoOj&index=11.
85. The 4 Horsemen of Meaning | Bishop Barron, John Vervaeke, and
    Jonathan Pageau | JBP Podcast S4: E60
    https://www.youtube.com/watch?v=FCvQsqSCWjA&t=3582s.
86. 2017 Maps of Meaning 04: Marionettes and Individuals (Part 3)
    https://www.youtube.com/watch?v=bV16NEWld8Q&list=PL22J3Va
    eABQAT-0aSPq-OKOpQlHyR4k5h&index=4.

87. Islam, Christ, and Liberty | Mustafa Akyol | The JBP Podcast S4: E56
https://www.youtube.com/watch?v=9b8kprIQ-yo.

88. 2015 Maps of Meaning 10: Genesis I / Part 2 (Jordan Peterson)
https://www.youtube.com/watch?v=sJVtAIIHxu0&list=PL22J3VaeA
BQByVcW4lXQ46glULC-ekhOp&index=20.

89. 2015 Maps of Meaning 11: Genesis II / Part 1 (Jordan Peterson)
https://www.youtube.com/watch?v=Q_2UYIuvDXI&list=PL22J3Vae
ABQByVcW4lXQ46glULC-ekhOp&index=21.

90. 2015 Maps of Meaning 11: Conclusion - The Hero / Part 2 (Jordan
Peterson)
https://www.youtube.com/watch?v=G7U9el_yVhI&list=PL22J3Vae
ABQByVcW4lXQ46glULC-ekhOp&index=22.

91. 2016 Lecture 09 Maps of Meaning: Genesis
https://www.youtube.com/watch?v=Gacjj2aCo7Q&list=PL22J3VaeA
BQAGbKJNDrRa6GNL0iL4KoOj&index=13.

92. 2016 Lecture 10 Maps of Meaning: Gautama Buddha, Adam and Eve
https://www.youtube.com/watch?v=F7T5cg1a77A&list=PL22J3VaeA
BQAGbKJNDrRa6GNL0iL4KoOj&index=14.

93. 2017 Maps of Meaning 10: Genesis and the Buddha
https://www.youtube.com/watch?v=7XtEZvLo-Sc&list=PL22J3VaeA
BQAT-0aSPq-OKOpQlHyR4k5h&index=10.

94. Biblical Series I: Introduction to the Idea of God
https://www.youtube.com/watch?v=f-wWBGo6a2w&list=PL22J3Vae
ABQD_IZs7y60I3lUrrFTzkpat.

95. 2017 Maps of Meaning 11: The Flood and the Tower
https://www.youtube.com/watch?v=T4fjSrVCDvA&list=PL22J3Vae
ABQAT-0aSPq-OKOpQlHyR4k5h&index=11.

96. 2017 Maps of Meaning 12: Final: The Divinity of the Individual
https://www.youtube.com/watch?v=6V1eMvGGcXQ&list=PL22J3
VaeABQAT-0aSPq-OKOpQlHyR4k5h&index=12.

97. Biblical Series II: Genesis 1: Chaos & Order
https://www.youtube.com/watch?v=hdrLQ7DpiWs&list=PL22J3Vae
ABQD_IZs7y60I3lUrrFTzkpat&index=2.

98. Biblical Series III: God and the Hierarchy of Authority
https://www.youtube.com/watch?v=R_GPAl_q2QQ&list=PL22J3Vae
ABQD_IZs7y60I3lUrrFTzkpat&index=3.

99. Biblical Series IV: Adam and Eve: Self-Consciousness, Evil, and Death
https://www.youtube.com/watch?v=Ifi5KkXig3s&list=PL22J3VaeAB QD_IZs7y60I3lUrrFTzkpat&index=4.

100. Biblical Series V: Cain and Abel: The Hostile Brothers
https://www.youtube.com/watch?v=44f3mxcsI50&list=PL22J3VaeA BQD_IZs7y60I3lUrrFTzkpat&index=5.

101. Biblical Series VI: The Psychology of the Flood
https://www.youtube.com/watch?v=wNjbasba-Qw&list=PL22J3Vae ABQD_IZs7y60I3lUrrFTzkpat&index=6.

102. Biblical Series VII: Walking with God: Noah and the Flood (corrected)
https://www.youtube.com/watch?v=6gFjB9FTN58&list=PL22J3Vae ABQD_IZs7y60I3lUrrFTzkpat&index=7.

103. Background to Lecture VIII: Abrahamic Stories, with Matthieu & Jonathan Pageau
https://www.youtube.com/watch?v=f3vqXCLhJLE&list=PL22J3VaeA BQD_IZs7y60I3lUrrFTzkpat&index=8.

104. The Death and Resurrection of Christ: A Commentary in Five Parts
https://www.youtube.com/watch?v=xPIanlF6IwM&list=PL22J3VaeA BQD_IZs7y60I3lUrrFTzkpat&index=17.

105. Beacon Press: *Man's Search for Meaning*
http://www.beacon.org/Mans-Search-for-Meaning-P602. aspx#:~:text=This%20seminal%20book%2C%20which%20 has,sold%20over%2016%20million%20copies.

106. 2015 Personality Lecture 13: Existentialism: Nazi Germany and the USSR
https://www.youtube.com/watch?v=XY7a1RXMbHI&list=PL22J3Va eABQAhrMCQUa6sde_Y9DVbLYRv&index=12.

107. 2015 Personality Lecture 14: Existentialism: Solzhenitsyn / Intro to Biology & Psychometrics
https://www.youtube.com/watch?v=wZnqLvLbLV0&list=PL22J3Vae ABQAhrMCQUa6sde_Y9DVbLYRv&index=13.

108. 2016 Personality Lecture 08: Existentialism: Nietzsche, Dostoevsky and Social Hierarchy
https://www.youtube.com/watch?v=WjpV9mja3Wc&list=PL22J3Vae ABQAOhH1CLMNnMl2R-O1abW1T&index=8.

109. 2017 Personality 13: Existentialism via Solzhenitsyn and the Gulag
https://www.youtube.com/watch?v=w84uRYq0Uc8&list=PL22J3Vae
ABQApSdW8X7lIhe34eKN6XhCi&index=11.

110. If You Struggle To Find Meaning In Your Life, Watch This
https://www.youtube.com/watch?app=desktop&v=sLLyWBySGwg.

111. Kali
(Fig. 8.4) *Maps of Meaning*, 162.
(Fig 8.5) Stock image.

112. F. Nietzsche, *The Will To Power*, trans. W. Kaufmann and R. J.
Hollingdale (New York: Vintage, 1880/2011); *Beyond Order*, 162.

113. Piaget, J. (1962). Play, dreams, and imitation in childhood. New
York: W.W. Norton.

114. Selective Attention Test
http://www.dansimons.com/videos.html.

115. 2017 Personality 08: Carl Jung and the Lion King (Part 2)
https://www.youtube.com/watch?v=X6pbJTqv2hw&list=PL22J3Vae
ABQApSdW8X7lIhe34eKN6XhCi&index=6.

116. The Perfect Mode of Being | Jonathan Pageau - Jordan B. Peterson
Podcast S4: E8
https://www.youtube.com/watch?v=2rAqVmZwqZM&t=1304s.

117. Apsu & Tiamat
(Fig. 10.1) Artist sketch.
(Fig. 10.2) Stock image.
(Fig. 10.3) Stock image.

118. Ouroboros
(Fig. 8.2) Stock image.
(Fig. 8.3) Engraving of a wyvern-type ouroboros by Lucas Jennis, in
the 1625 alchemical tract *De Lapide Philosophico*.

119. Horus
(Fig. 11.1) Artist sketch.
(Fig. 11.2) Stock image.

120. "This is not a pipe" - Rene Magritte
https://en.wikipedia.org/wiki/The_Treachery_of_Images.

121. The story of the Two Wolves
https://www.huffpost.com/entry/do-you-feed-the-good-wolf_b_804
8124.

122. *Man's Search for Meaning*
     Frankl, Viktor. *Man's Search for Meaning: An introduction to logother-
     apy*. Boston, Massachusetts: Beacon Press, (2006).

123. *12 Rules for Life*
     Peterson, Jordan. *12 Rules for Life: An Antidote to Chaos*. Toronto,
     Canada: Penguin Random House Canada, (2018).

124. *Beyond Order*
     Peterson, Jordan. *Beyond Order: 12 More Rules for Life*. Toronto,
     Canada: Penguin Random House Canada, (2021).

125. *Maps of Meaning*
     Peterson, Jordan. *Maps of Meaning: The Architecture of Belief.* New
     York, New York: Routledge, (1999).

126. *The Gulag Archipelago*
     Solzhenitsyn, Aleksandr. *The Gulag Archipelago, 1918-56: An ex-
     periment in literary investigation* (T.P. Whitney, Trans.). New York:
     Harper and Row.
     (1974). *Vol. 1. The gulag archipelago.*
     (1975). *Vol. 2. The gulag archipelago two.*
     (1978). *Vol. 3. The gulag archipelago three.*

# Endnotes

1   *Maps of Meaning*, quoting *The Gay Science*, 7.
2   *Beyond Order*, referencing The Will to Power, 162.
3   Source 26 - 9:40.
4   Source 42 - 1:23:30.
5   Source 26 - 11:03.
6   Piaget, J. (1962). *Play, Dreams, and Imitation in Childhood*. New York: W.W. Norton.
7   Source 23 - 20:13.
8   Source 23 - 14:00.
9   Source 24 - 55:00.
10  Source 24 - 57:14.
11  Source 24 - 56:12.
12  *Maps of Meaning*, 93.
13  Source 23 - 30:25.
14  *Maps of Meaning*, 73.
15  Source 26 - 6:24.
16  *Maps of Meaning*, 77.
17  Recreated from *Maps of Meaning*, 80.
18  *Maps of Meaning*, 78.
19  Source 1 - 1:33.
20  Source 1 - 3:59.
21  *Maps of Meaning*, 138–139.
22  Source 1 - 9:10.
23  Source 42 - 1:26:02.
24  Source 42 - 1:35:31.
25  Source 2 - 19:27.
26  *Maps of Meaning*, 22.
27  This idea is discussed further in *The Ecological Approach to Visual Perception* by James J. Gibson.
28  Source 2 - 25:40.
29  Source 2 - 25:47, Source 2 - 27:35, Source 40 - 47:40.
30  Reformulated from Source 2 - 7:20, Source 59 - 1:07:07.
31  *Beyond Order*, 60.
32  Reformulated from: Source 2 - 24:16, Source 58 - 1:24:26.
33  Source 58 - 1:25:48.
34  Source 41 - 13:11.
35  *Beyond Order*, 65; Source 4 - 1:15:30.
36  Source 5 - 26:12.
37  Source 6 - 9:21.

38  *12 Rules for Life*, 209.
39  Source 6 - 24:52.
40  Source 7 - 8:15.
41  Source 7 - 9:20.
42  Source 7 - 17: 33.
43  Source 7 - 10:23.
44  Source 7 - 52:19.
45  Source 7 - 24:09.
46  Source 4 - 1:16:24.
47  Source 7 - 30:00.
48  Source 10 - 37:10.
49  Source 7 - 47:55.
50  Source 7 - 50:15.
51  Source 6 - 26:47.
52  Source 7 - 49:24.
53  Source 106 - 1:15:39.
54  Source 102 - 25:17, Source 109 - 9:17, Source 109 - 1:40:15.
55  *12 Rules for Life*, 212.
56  Source 66 - 30:46.
57  *The Gulag Archipelago*, 325–326.
58  Source 92 - 1:32:27, Source 77 - 33:18.
59  Source 107 - 59:38, Source 109 - 1:37:55.
60  Source 7 - 32:50.
61  Source 7 - 28:20; *12 Rules for Life*, 157–158.
62  Kaufmann, W. (Ed. and Trans.). (1975). *Existentialism from Dostoevsky to Sartre*. New York: Meridian, 122–123.
63  Source 97 - 1:08:56; *The Gulag Archipelago*, 313.
64  Source 13 - 22:18.
65  Source 13 - 23:34.
66  Source 13 - 24:17.
67  Source 25 - 3:24, Source 26 - 15:55.
68  Source 27 - 1:05:48.
69  J. Panksepp, *Affective Neuroscience: The Foundations of Human and Animal Emotions* [New York: Oxford University Press, 1998], 280–299.
70  Source 26 - 1:41:00.
71  *Beyond Order*, 5.
72  Source 24 - 1:07:30, Source 25 - 1:08:03.
73  Source 98 - 1:23:10.
74  Source 24 - 15:47.
75  Source 24 - 20:31; *Beyond Order*,10.
76  Source 26 - 20:46.
77  *12 Rules for Life*, 163.
78  *12 Rules for Life*, 34.
79  *Maps of Meaning*, 108.
80  *Maps of Meaning*, 15.
81  Source 114.
82  *12 Rules for Life*, 96–97.
83  Source 49 - 26:43.
84  *Maps of Meaning*, 101.
85  *Maps of Meaning*, 23.
86  Source 64 - 8:33.
87  Source 43 - 2:00:05.

# Endnotes

88    Source 55 - 55:27.
89    Source 43 - 2:01:37, Source 55 - 59:07, Source 59 - 1:01:30.
90    *Maps of Meaning*, 43.
91    Source 99 - 16:07.
92    *Maps of Meaning*, 69.
93    *Maps of Meaning*, 68–69.
94    *Maps of Meaning*, 48, 52.
95    Source 33 - 21:18.
96    *Maps of Meaning*, 73–74.
97    Source 33 - 25:21.
98    Source 37 - 56:55.
99    Source 38 - 42:35.
100   Source 28 - 41:58.
101   Source 43 - 1:22:33.
102   Source 29 - 48:31.
103   Source 94 - 21:52.
104   Source 94 - 38:30.
105   *Maps of Meaning*, 95.
106   *Maps of Meaning*, 95, citing Roger Brown's Social Psychology: The Second Edition.
107   Section paraphrased from *Maps of Meaning*, 96–97, which was based on the work of George Lakoff.
108   *Maps of Meaning*, 97.
109   *Maps of Meaning*, 97.
110   *Maps of Meaning*, 97.
111   *Maps of Meaning*, 97.
112   *12 Rules for Life*, 36.
113   *12 Rules for Life*, 40.
114   *12 Rules for Life*, 35.
115   Source 51 - 43:36, Source 97 - 28:48.
116   Source 51 - 47:31.
117   *Maps of Meaning*, 194–195.
118   *Beyond Order*, 308–309.
119   *Beyond Order*, 68-69; Source 34 - 1:58:57.
120   *12 Rules for Life*, 39.
121   Source 66 - 1:29:54.
122   Source 58 - 1:23:03.
123   Source 118.
124   *12 Rules for Life*, 11.
125   Source 61 - 37:05.
126   Source 55 - 42:03.
127   *Beyond Order*, 79 (footnote).
128   Source 68 - 30:09.
129   Source 75 - 44:46.
130   Source 76 - 1:51:14.
131   Source 60 - 21:04.
132   *12 Rules for Life*, 40.
133   Source 31 - 42:03, Source 70 - 1:13:21.
134   *12 Rules for Life*, 302.
135   *Maps of Meaning*, 208-209.
136   *Maps of Meaning*, 213.
137   *Maps of Meaning*, 379.
138   Source 83 - 34:46.

139 *Maps of Meaning*, 156–157.
140 *Maps of Meaning*, 148–149, citing Erich Neumann in *The Great Mother: An Analysis of the Archetype*.
141 *Maps of Meaning*, 161, citing Erich Neumann in *The Great Mother: An Analysis of the Archetype*.
142 *Maps of Meaning*, 163.
143 *Maps of Meaning*, 154–155.
144 *Maps of Meaning*, 161–162.
145 Source 111.
146 Source 61 - 50:02, Source 84 - 16:04.
147 Source 61 - 49:21.
148 *Maps of Meaning*, 166.
149 *Maps of Meaning*, 164.
150 *Maps of Meaning*, 166.
151 Source 62 - 20:30.
152 *Maps of Meaning*, 202–203.
153 *Beyond Order*, 79.
154 Source 66 - 22:17.
155 Source 92 - 2:46:21.
156 Source 31 - 41:31.
157 *Maps of Meaning*, 185.
158 *Maps of Meaning*, 308.
159 *Maps of Meaning*, 327.
160 *Beyond Order*, 41–42.
161 *Maps of Meaning*, 181.
162 *Maps of Meaning*, 182–183.
163 *Maps of Meaning*, 184 taken from Bellini, J.
164 *Maps of Meaning*, 183–184.
165 Source 36 - 41:42.
166 Source 76 - 1:24:19.
167 Source 76 - 1:28:31; *Beyond Order*, 78–79.
168 Source 34 - 56:18.
169 Source 76 - 1:29:54.
170 Source 76 - 1:129:01.
171 Source 65 - 38:41.
172 *Maps of Meaning*, 166.
173 *Maps of Meaning*, 180.
174 Source 68 - 1:00:26, Source 69 - 6:40.
175 *Maps of Meaning*, 316.
176 *Maps of Meaning*, 314; Source 31 - 34:22.
177 Source 74 - 45:17, Source 74 - 57:38.
178 *12 Rules for Life*, 229.
179 Source 77 - 5:05.
180 Source 77 - 11:34.
181 Source 42 - 32:10.
182 Source 43 - 1:39:47.
183 Source 42 - 33:03.
184 Source 77 - 13:51.
185 Source 42 - 25:56; Panzram: *Butchering Humanity: An Autobiography*.
186 Source 42 - 23:29.
187 Source 80 - 0:08.
188 Source 117.

189 Source 81 - Tablet 1:69–77.
190 Source 81 - Tablet 1:131–158.
191 Source 81 - Tablet 1:95–98.
192 Source 80 - 19:17.
193 Source 79 - 17:27.
194 Source 81 - Tablet 4:95–104.
195 Source 98 - 2:01:42.
196 *Beyond Order*, 73–74.
197 *Beyond Order*, 72.
198 Source 80 - 29:28.
199 *Maps of Meaning*, 127.
200 Source 60 - 1:12:34; *Beyond Order*, 73.
201 Source 82 - 12:23.
202 Source 101 - 20:42.
203 Source 83 - 1:09:22.
204 Source 115 - 49:18.
205 Source 82 - 21:09.
206 Source 83 - 1:21:58, Source 41 - 21:54.
207 Source 119.
208 Source 82 - 26:11.
209 Source 76 - 2:06:47.
210 *Beyond Order*, 122–123.
211 Source 83 - 1:31:32.
212 Source 83 - 1:03:12.
213 Source 82 - 28:20.
214 Source 29 - 52:39.
215 Source 63 - 26:59, Source 76 - 1:31:13.
216 Source 76 - 2:08:16.
217 Source 60 - 2:18:39.
218 Source 82 - 31:18.
219 Source 93 - 54:11.
220 *Maps of Meaning*, 110; Source 93 - 1:20:27; *Beyond Order*, 258.
221 Source 93 - 1:18:18.
222 Genesis 1:10, 12, 18, 25, 31.
223 Source 97 - 2:14:19.
224 Genesis 3:1.
225 Genesis 3:2–3.
226 Genesis 3:4–5.
227 *Beyond Order*, 114.
228 Source 89 - 39:47.
229 Source 91 - 9:47.
230 Source 93 - 2:02:50.
231 Source 89 - 1:30:49.
232 Source 77 - 21:08.
233 Source 99 - 2:00:46.
234 Source 93 - 1:52:48.
235 Source 99 - 2:01:42.
236 Source 89 - 1:36:36.
237 Genesis 4:1–4.
238 *12 Rules for Life*, 165–166.
239 Source 100 - 1:07:27.
240 Source 99 - 40:09.

241   Source 90 - 9:11.

242   Source 90 - 9:29.

243   Source 90 - 9:50.

244   Source 90 - 11:35, Source 90 - 14:48.

245   Genesis 4:8.

246   Source 95 - 1:11:20.

247   Genesis 4:11–17.

248   Genesis 4:23–24.

249   Genesis 4:22.

250   Genesis 6:8–9.

251   Source 101 - 18:08.

252   Source 83 - 1:06:41.

253   Source 101 - 1:54:16; *12 Rules for Life*, 157.

254   Source 95 - 1:46:58.

255   Source 101 - 1:56:20.

256   Source 29 - 24:44.

257   Luke 1:26–38.

258   Luke 2:1–7.

259   Luke 2:52.

260   Luke 3:21–22.

261   Matthew 3:11.

262   Matthew 3:16–17.

263   Matthew 4:1.

264   *12 Rules for Life*, 181.

265   1 John 4:16.

266   *12 Rules for Life*, 181–182.

267   *Maps of Meaning*, 343.

268   *The Gulag Archipelago*, 58–59.

269   *Maps of Meaning*, 346. citing *The Gulag Archipelago*.

270   *Man's Search for Meaning*, 26–27.

271   *Man's Search for Meaning*, 30–32.

272   *The Gulag Archipelago*, 315.

273   *Maps of Meaning*, 346, citing *The Gulag Archipelago*, 302.

274   *Man's Search for Meaning*, 4–5.

275   *Maps of Meaning*, 354, citing *Man's Search for Meaning*, 5.

276   *Maps of Meaning*, 354, citing *Man's Search for Meaning* 4.

277   *Maps of Meaning*, 355, citing *The Gulag Archipelago*.

278   *The Gulag Archipelago*, 307.

279   *The Gulag Archipelago*, 317–319.

280   *Maps of Meaning*, 350–351.

281   *Maps of Meaning*, 353, citing *The Gulag Archipelago*.

282   *Man's Search for Meaning*, 86.

283   *The Gulag Archipelago*, 312.

284   *Man's Search for Meaning*, 65–67.

285   *Maps of Meaning*, 332–333.

286   *Maps of Meaning*, 469, citing *The Gospel of Thomas*, Sayings 1–6.

287   Mark 10:52.

288   Mark 5:34.

289   Matthew 8:10.

290   Matthew 8:13.

291   Matthew 17:20–21.

292   Matthew 14:31.

293 Mark 6:5-6.
294 Source 87 - 47:33.
295 *Beyond Order*, 45–46.
296 Luke 7:30.
297 John 12:4-6.
298 Matthew 26:14–15.
299 Luke 22:44.
300 Matthew 26:56; Mark 14:50.
301 Matthew 26:65–66.
302 Matthew 27:46.
303 *Beyond Order*, 361-363.
304 Luke 23:46.
305 Matthew 28:19–20.
306 Mark 16:19.
307 *12 Rules for Life*, 189–190.
308 Source 97 - 1:24:55.
309 Source 96 - 2:07:38.
310 Colossians 1:15.
311 Source 116 - 21:44.
312 *Man's Search for Meaning*, 76–77.
313 *Man's Search for Meaning*, 109.
314 *Man's Search for Meaning*, 108–109.
315 *Man's Search for Meaning*, 79–80.
316 *Man's Search for Meaning*, 138.
317 *Man's Search for Meaning*, 111-112.
318 *Man's Search for Meaning*, XV-XVI.
319 Source 110 - 0:20.
320 Source 59 - 1:29:30; *Beyond Order*, 136–137.
321 *Maps of Meaning*, 447.
322 Source 84 - 1:33.
323 Source 84 - 5:45.
324 *Man's Search for Meaning*, 118.
325 Source 120.
326 Source 5 - 53:05.
327 Romans 1:21–23.